THE ROYAL CHATEAUX
OF THE ILE-DE-FRANCE

by Jacques   Levron

POMPADOUR

translated by Claire Eliane Engel

(London, George Allen & Unwin, 1963)

THE ROYAL CHATEAUX
OF THE
ILE-DE-FRANCE

JACQUES LEVRON

TRANSLATED BY CLAIRE-ELIANE ENGEL

RAND McNALLY & COMPANY

CHICAGO · NEW YORK · SAN FRANCISCO

CONTENTS

INTRODUCTION

VERSAILLES, Fontainebleau, St Germain, Compiègne, and Rambouillet: these royal castles encircle the capital of France like a splendid necklace. Visitors to Paris go from one to the other, unaware of the ties between them during centuries of history, despite their widely different styles. Obviously, there is a striking contrast between the shaky tower of Etampes and the Palace of Versailles, or between the manor of Villers-Cotterêts and the fortress of Gisors. Yet all four have one thing in common: they were built to house and protect the king, the royal family and their companions.

Of course, there were royal chateaux in the other provinces of France. Those along the Loire were the cherished homes of the Valois; it was the same in Berry, where Louis XI owned the fine fortress of Mehun-sur-Yèvre, and in Provence and Béarn after they had become French. Even far from Paris there are estates that belonged to the crown, but the Ile-de-France and the Valois can boast of more royal chateaux than any other region.

It is easy to explain so large a number. When the Capetians made Paris their capital, they did not abandon one of the characteristics of their dynasty: its vagrant habit. They were, after all, merely following in the footsteps of the Merovingians. If these kings showed a tendency to roam from one estate to another, it was for reasons of simple economic necessity. When they had consumed the resources of one, they had to take to the road again – even if it was only a very bad road – to seek another residence.

The Capetians had other reasons for moving about their estates. From Hugues Capet to Philip the Fair, they all understood the vital importance of being always on the spot. They knew how vital it was to show themselves to their subjects. Their cavalcades through a still narrow territory reinforced the somewhat shaky loyalty of their vassals; they made it possible for small tenants to approach the king and to tell him their troubles; they also enabled the sovereign to see the state of his castles for himself and to see to their upkeep. They were interesting also from another point of view: they gave the king the opportunity to indulge in the favourite royal pastime of hunting.

All the French kings, from Hugues Capet to Louis XVI, were great hunters. And it must be admitted that no French forests were better provided with game of all sorts than those around Paris. Even today, in spite of the serious deforestation which has taken place, where can we find more beautiful woodland landscapes than in the forests of St Germain-en-Laye, Fontainebleau or Compiègne? And the deep criticism of Louis XIV by his courtiers for eventually selecting Versailles as the site of his palace was precisely that, as distinct from other royal chateaux, it had no surrounding forest.

The first royal residences, early in the Middle Ages, also protected the roads to the capital, thanks to their powerful defences. They were not always very comfortable: but the King did feel secure in them, and was able at the same time to hunt from his own doorstep.

The Hundred Years War for a time compelled the Valois to leave the banks of the Seine and migrate towards the Loire. As soon as the enemy had been driven from the Ile-de-France they returned to Paris. Yet in their hearts they kept a soft spot for some of their residences and in the sixteenth century Chambord, Blois and others, rebuilt and enlarged according to the taste of the period, were often visited by the court. As for the royal chateaux around Paris, they benefited, too, by the new taste, and Fontainebleau and St Germain-en-Laye, among others, are Renaissance masterpieces.

Centuries passed, but the habits of the court did not change. It is usually thought that under Louis XIV the royal household stayed at Versailles. It is partly true, but it is easily forgotten that Louis XIV also stayed at St Germain, Marly, Fontainebleau, or at St Cloud at his brother's chateau. And Louis XV followed the ways of his great-grandfather exactly. The police superintendent of Versailles, Narbonne, made a list of the King's trips in 1739: twenty days at Marly, fifty-three at Fontainebleau, fifty-three at Compiègne, fourteen at Rambouillet and so on. He was at Versailles for only 190 days. Louis XV probably hoped that by this procedure he might succeed in escaping from himself and his overwhelming boredom. Anyhow, those endless journeys helped to keep the royal chateaux in trim and to induce architects to alter them and keep them up-to-date. The Marquis de Pompadour at Bellevue and Mme du Barry at Louveciennes helped and protected artists and made their fortunes.

Financial difficulties compelled Louis XVI to cut down expenses. He stopped caring for several chateaux on the royal estates and he even thought of selling some of them or turning them into more useful buildings. Several chateaux were pulled down or turned into barracks. And yet the finest palaces were not only cared for but embellished during his reign, and it was not only at Versailles that Petits Appartements were planned and decorated for Marie-Antoinette, but also at Fontainebleau and Compiègne.

The Revolution was less destructive than one would have thought, where the palaces had become national property. Certainly there were losses and there was destruction; yet, with a few exceptions nothing was put beyond repair. Throughout the nineteenth century the reigning dynasties zealously – far too zealously sometimes – guarded their artistic heirlooms, some of which bore the mark of the private tastes and preferences of the rulers.

It is needless to emphasize the effect upon French art of the centuries-long royal care for the chateaux around Paris. It is usual to follow the example of the sovereign and so, during the Renaissance, several chateaux were built along the lines laid down by the architect Philibert Delorme when he built Fontainebleau for Henri II, and the setting of that palace was a model followed by many artists. As for Versailles, according to Bernard Champigneulle, no building in the world, since antiquity, has been such a source of inspiration and imitation for architects and decorators. Similarly, how many copies of the Petit Trianon and the Hameau were scattered all over France by the end of the eighteenth century by noblemen who liked to have, in their own provincial parks, the Versailles atmosphere which their financial difficulties had compelled them to forsake?

Similar consequences can be observed in landscape gardening. Le Notre has been imitated all over France. The parks which owe their harmonious lay-out to him are numerous, and 'English' gardens became the fashion in the next century, starting a new craze because they had been admired at court.

This book is an attempt to tell the story of those royal parks and chateaux. Sometimes the visitor does not quite appreciate the richness of some of the most celebrated palaces. We have tried to help him to grasp it. The unity of this book comes from this very selection: buildings which at one time or another have belonged to the crown and have all afforded a background to the history of France.

J.L.

CHAPTER I

FROM THE FEUDAL FORTRESS TO THE RENAISSANCE CHATEAU

OF THE feudal fortresses of Montlhéry, Etampes, Gisors or Dourdan it is difficult to discover which is the oldest. They were all founded in the Middle Ages and they all became parts of the royal estate at an early date. Their vicissitudes are part of French history. Today they have something in common in that they are mere skeletons of bare stone emerging from briar and bracken.

Montlhéry stands as a watch-tower at the outskirts of Paris. From the top of the high round tower, all that is left of a once powerful fortress, Montmartre and the hills surrounding the city can be seen.

> La dame est à Montmartre, regarde la vallée,
> Voit de Montlhéry la grant tour crénelée. . . .[1]

wrote the poet of *Berte aux grands piés*. Tristan Klingsor's[2] lovely ballad is almost an echo:

> Sur la tour de Montlhéry
> Un joli jouvencel est monté,
> Un joli jouvencel de Paris.[3]

Thibault, nicknamed File-Etoupe, the second son of Bouchard de Montmorency, as early as the beginning of the eleventh century built a castle at the top of the hill. He established his dominion over the whole surrounding country. It was better to be with him than against him, for the restless feudal lord was not over-scrupulous. His descendants were not much better; his great-grandson Guy II was nicknamed Trousçel, the Highwayman, and he well deserved it. He was coarse and brutal, his lordly neighbours dreaded him and even the King of France himself – admittedly the very insignificant Philip I – had often to fight when crossing his vassal's fiefs on his way to Orleans. Finally, in 1104 he got

[1] The lady from Montmartre looks across the valley and sees the great crenelated tower of Montlhéry . . .
[2] Contemporary French poet. His poem has been set to music by Francis Poulenc.
[3] On the tower of Montlhéry stands a pretty youth, a handsome youth from Paris.

13

the better of Trousçel. Shortly before he died, the King said to his son Louis: 'Look well after this tower: it aged me before my time. The guile and wickedness of those who dwell there never gave me a moment's rest.' Yet it was only in 1118 that Montlhéry was finally taken from Hugues de Crécy, to whom it had been entrusted by Louis VI.

Henceforth Montlhéry belonged to the King, and a provost kept it for him. The Capetians often stayed there, for it was a stage on the road to Languedoc. They attended to the upkeep of its walls, rebuilt the ramparts and felt secure within its keep. This became obvious in 1227.

At that time, Blanche of Castille, St Louis' mother, ruled the kingdom for her thirteen-year-old son, and the barons did not like her. According to the Capetian tradition, the young King had gone from Paris to Orleans to show himself to his subjects. He had but a small retinue with him. The barons met at Corbeil and decided to kidnap him in order to oppose Blanche. As luck would have it, rumours of the plot reached Louis' ears as he was riding peacefully back towards Paris. With perfect sang-froid, he rode to Montlhéry and at the same time had his mother warned of what was afoot.

The touching scene that followed has come down to us through Joinville. As soon as they knew that the King was threatened, the Parisians rushed out. Led by a few knights, with troops riding with ensigns flying, men, women and children hurried along the Orleans road, and were soon strung out all along it. 'From Montlhéry to Paris,' wrote Joinville, 'the road was filled with armed or unarmed people, all of them shouting: "Noel! Noel! May the Lord give a long life to our King! May He protect him from his enemies! Noel! Noel!" '

From afar, the barons heard what was happening. There was nothing left then but to disperse discomforted. The fortress of Montlhéry had played its part well as a royal bastion in the Paris region.

About two centuries later Englishmen and Burgundians learned the importance of that role. The old fortress, somewhat repaired and rearmed, was still a threat to those who did not occupy it. In 1358 it had been besieged by the English without avail. Edward III conquered it in 1360, after a brave fight by Captain Jean de Hangest. The French troops reconquered it, and partisans of Armagnac and Burgundy continued to fight over it for ten years. In 1423 it was conquered again by the English, who kept it till 1438.

The castle suffered much through those furious struggles. By the end of the fourteenth century it had already been repaired. In the reign of Louis XI it once again played a part in French history. In 1465, claiming they were fighting for the welfare of the realm—a rather strange notion of it! – the French nobility rebelled against the King once more. Summoned by the Comte de Charolais, who was later to be known as Charles the Bold, the rebellious lords rode towards Paris and occupied the town of Montlhéry. Louis XI, returning from Auvergne, turned back and fought them in the plain of Longpont, on Tuesday, July 16th.

It was a long and desultory battle. Finally, both armies withdrew, each claiming victory, towards Corbeil on one side, Etampes on the other. The fortress had held out for the King, but the town had been partly burnt, and Louis XI forgot to repay the loss sustained by its inhabitants.

By that time the use of artillery was depriving the castles of much of their importance. Yet in that part of Ile-de-France which was a battlefield for League partisans and Huguenots during the Wars of Religion, Montlhéry was once more the key to several battles. It was captured in 1562 by the Prince de Condé and the Calvinists, and assaulted again later, under Henri III. Consequently, after the peace it endured the fate of most medieval fortresses: it was pulled down. In 1603 Henri IV allowed Jérome le Maistre, Lord of Bellejambe, to use its stones to repair his own castle.

Montlhéry was a ruin. The King rented it to some high dignitaries for a large sum of money: it went to the Lamoignons and the Phélippeaux. Its last owner was Marshal de Mouchy, Comte de Noailles, who was beheaded during the Terror.

The keep, which was all that was left of the old fortress, was put to some use. It was too well situated not to serve for scientific experiments; as early as 1738 it served to measure the speed of sound. A century later, Fresnel went there to measure the speed of light (1822). A Chappe telegraph was placed on its summit in 1825, and during the last war the Germans used it as a radio station for military purposes.

Today, for many people, Montlhéry means only a motor racing track, but to travellers coming from the south the tower soars above the road as a sign of the nearby capital. Only archaeologists will stoop to find traces of the four ramparts which once surrounded the citadel, identify the foundations of the four big towers and the remains of the old guard-room. The ordinary visitor will merely roam in the powerful keep which saw so many royal processions pass during the centuries.

Along the same road to Languedoc and Spain which took pilgrims to Santiago de Compostela, and four miles south of Montlhéry, we find the tower of Guinette d'Etampes.

Guinette: the name has a pert and lively ring that contrasts with its austere walls. As a matter of fact, it means *guignette*, the tower from which one surveys (*guigne*) the surrounding countryside: in fact a watch-tower. It was part of the fortifications covering the hill and defending the city. A miniature in the *Très riches heures du Duc de Berry*[1] enables us to see what this powerful fortress looked like.

In the eleventh century there was already a castle at Etampes-le-Chastel[2].

---

[1] A beautiful illuminated manuscript of the fifteenth century, kept at Chantilly.
[2] From *The Chronicles of Helgaud*, a French monk who lived in the eleventh century.

15

Philippe-Auguste built the keep by the end of the twelfth century. For a time he used it to imprison his first wife, the pitiful Ingeborg; this lovely Danish princess was unlucky enough to displease her husband on their wedding night and he could never master his hatred for her. For years Philippe dragged her from castle to castle and from convent to convent, which were only so many prisons until the day when the Pope, in the name of the Church, compelled him to take her back and treat her at least as a queen, if not as his wife. But by this time the poor woman's martyrdom had lasted twenty years.

In the thirteenth century the first floor of the keep was ornamented with pointed arches which still survive. The second floor is stranger: it contains two diaphragmatic arches which cross each other. At the top of the tower is a small turret serving as a watch-tower. The layout of the Guinette tower is quadrifoil. Dom Fleureau, the good seventeenth century historian of Etampes, once wrote: 'The keep was built in the shape of a four-leaved rose, forty *toises*[1] around and twenty in height; the walls were twelve feet thick, and there was a *pied-droit* staircase set into them to give access to the upper storeys of the tower, above which rose a turret used as a watch-tower from which the surrounding fields and roads could be observed. There was a well, reaching as high as the first floor of the tower. All these buildings were covered with slates and lead, decorated with roses, and other architectural designs.'

After three centuries, this description is still not inaccurate. One still finds traces of the staircase described by Dom Fleureau, the well, the big vaulted hall on the first floor and the one on the second floor, which was the commanding officer's apartment. The roses and ornamentations have vanished, destroyed during the battles and assaults which the tower sustained.

And yet it was not war, but the inhabitants' will which entailed the castle's destruction. After the civil wars of the sixteenth century they took the opportunity of Henri IV's visit to his city to beg his permission to destroy the tower which had given them so much trouble. The Vert-Galant agreed. Immediately, they heaped powder casks in the tower. After the explosion nothing remained but crumbling walls, and yet Guinette, in spite of many cracks, still survives.

It must be admitted that the people of Etampes had valid reasons to look askance at the castle that dominated their city. During the Hundred Years War, like the castle of Montlhéry, it was the scene of violent struggles. The histories of these two fortresses have many points in common: when one fell, the other did not hold out for long. At the beginning of the fifteenth century Etampes was the scene of violent battles between the people of Armagnac and Burgundy. In 1411 the Duke of Burgundy besieged the fortress, then held for the Armagnacs by Jean de Bosredon. The city had opened its gate to the Burgundian army, for the castle had capitulated; but Jean de Bosredon, beleaguered in the keep with

[1] One *toise* equals approximately 6 2/5 English feet.

16

some of the soldiers and even several women and girls, refused to yield, and after assaulting the citadel for several days the Burgundians were about to leave. A mere burgher, André Roussel, criticized them, so they renewed their attacks more skilfully. Feeling that he had lost and might be smoked out of his keep like a fox from his lair, Bosredon negotiated surrender. He was allowed to depart with flying colours; he emerged from the main gate of the castle, magnificently arrayed in a doublet of crimson velvet, studded with gold and gems. It is not difficult to understand why such a man appealed so much to the ladies of the place.

The castle of Etampes was not spared when battles raged at Montlhéry. It was conquered twice, first by the Huguenots, then by the soldiers of the League. The inhabitants of the town suffered at the hands of both: they were robbed, injured and raped.

The last fight to take place in the Guinette Tower was during the Fronde. Condé's army, with Marshal de Tavannes in command, occupied Etampes in 1652, while Turenne's troops, who were camping at Arpajon, were about to bar access to Paris. While Mlle de Montpensier, the beautiful supporter of the rebels, was handing out ribbons and medals to her brave fighters, Turenne attacked the town and the rebels scampered off at top speed across gardens and orchards. According to Dom Fleureau, 500 men surrendered, but the old keep continued to hold out. The royal army withdrew, the Fronde partisans re-occupied Etampes and this was the beginning of a second siege, which lasted for a fortnight. The young King Louis XIV visited Turenne's camp and was nearly injured by a cannon ball which a thoughtless gunner had carelessly fired. On June 7th Turenne had to trot off in a hurry, summoned to another battlefield, and Marshal de Tavannes remained victorious. Shortly afterwards he withdrew, leaving Etampes in a rather derelict state.

At the end of the eighteenth century the royal keep was put to more peaceful uses. An adventurously-minded canon – his name was Desforges – built a flying machine and decided to try it from the top of the hill where the tower stands. It was a wicker-work cockpit covered with feathers and operated by oars which were likewise feathered. The results were uncertain. The canon fell to the ground injuring his elbow; he did not try again. However, he had succeeded in making his name known and that was probably all he wanted.

Far more dangerous flying machines bombed Guinette during the Second World War, but the old tower stood up to the attacks and, having been rather sketchily repaired, is still good for many centuries.

Montlhéry and Etampes epitomize for us the shaky beginnings of the Capetian monarchy fighting against the puny feudal lords of Ile-de-France. The long-standing rivalry between the Capetians and the Plantagenets gave birth to

Gisors. Some historians regard this rivalry as being a first Hundred Years War, more significant than the usual conflicts between lord and vassal.

This conflict was unavoidable from the very day when the dukes of Normandy, whose estates, after the treaty of 911, reached to the Epte, became kings of England. Compared with those powerful sovereigns, Louis VI (the Fat) and Louis VII were rather tame. It was only thanks to the powerful personality and good fortune of Philippe Auguste that the situation changed. That is the meaning of twelfth century history and of Gisors.

At the time when William Rufus, the Conqueror's son, realized how important its position was, the castle was but an insignificant feudal building, vassal to the Archbishop of Rouen. It stood on a hill where the Epte, the Troesne and the Réveillon meet, commanding all the surrounding valleys. The King immediately entrusted Robert de Bellesme with the task of building a castle, of which nothing but some foundations remain. In point of fact, the present castle, with its big keep, its ramparts and twelve towers and two gates, does not date earlier than the second half of the twelfth century. Its first builders were Henry II and Philippe-Auguste, intent on conquering Gisors.

Yet Henry I Beauclerk, Henry II's father, had already done some work there. No feudal castle was ever quite finished. It was enlarged and altered, new fortifications were added to the earlier ones. It became a summary of military art through the ages.

Henry I entertained Pope Calixtus II at Gisors. The Supreme Pontif was trying to reconcile the Duke of Normandy and his suzerain lord. He succeeded, but peace was never long-lived. In 1144 Louis VII grabbed Gisors again. Fourteen years later the King of France was weak enough to sign a disastrous treaty with Henry II, according to which Gisors and the Norman Vexin became his daughter Marguerite's dowry; she was to marry the King of England's eldest son. Henry II immediately grabbed the Vexin. For over thirty years Gisors was occupied by the Plantagenets, who undertook the building of the keep and of the still-surviving ramparts.

The keep stands on an artificial mound in the middle of the fortress. It is a high, octagonal tower, encased in a stone armour pierced by a gate topped with a semi-circular arch, a typical feature of twelfth century military art. It may be that Léon Gautier had Gisors or Château-Gaillard in mind when he described the medieval castle in his book on the knighthood.[1] The walls of the ramparts, as well as those of the keep, are strengthened by heavy buttresses. The keep, built on an irregular octagonal layout, is twenty metres high, but it is now only an empty shell with a few fireplaces suspended over nothing. A stone staircase, hidden in the wall, leads to the platform. Another, in a side turret,

[1] Léon Gautier, *La Chevalerie.*

dates only from the fifteenth century. It seems likely that a part of the keep was repaired early in the thirteenth century after a fire.

In a corner of the inner courtyard, the ruins of St Thomas Becket's chapel call to mind one of the most dramatic episodes of Henry II's reign. According to tradition, Thomas à Becket, Archbishop of Canterbury, lived for some time in Gisors, while he was banished from Court and a refugee in France. One knows how he was murdered at the King's order on December 29, 1170. After doing a humiliating public penance in the cathedral of Avranches, Henry II endowed many pious foundations to show his repentance. That is why he had a chapel built in the castle of Gisors and dedicated to St Thomas after the martyred archbishop had been canonized.

The rivalry between Richard Coeur-de-Lion and Philippe-Auguste became most acute when the French king came back from the Crusade, having taken good care to leave his adversary overseas. As early as 1193, with the help of Richard's sons, he grabbed Gisors again. Freed from the German prison where he was detained by a mean adversary ('Take care: the Devil is loose again! . . .') Richard had but one thought: revenge. To compensate for the loss of Gisors, he had the celebrated Château-Gaillard built above the valley of the Seine. In 1198 he attacked once more: on September 28th the army of the French king and that of the King of England, Duke of Normandy, met at Courcelles, south of Gisors. Philippe-Auguste was not victorious but he succeeded in forcing his way through the English knights to take refuge in the castle; but when he rode over the wooden bridge across the Epte it broke and the King fell into the river. The Virgin rescued him in this great peril: he was fished out by a clerk, Guillaume le Melo's son. Once out of the water, Philippe-Auguste, fearing to be besieged in Gisors, rode back to Paris. Richard did not pursue him, and when he was killed at Chalus, in Limousin, the situation completely changed.

Yet, out of prudence, Philippe-Auguste had the castle made even stronger during the following years. He had a second rampart built, and three more towers, the Devil Tower, the Governor's Tower and the Prisoner's Tower.

The latter was probably altered in the fifteenth century, but it has kept its early aspect. Three stories vaulted with ogives are reached by a winding staircase. The highest room had a large chimney and a baking oven. In the middle room the provincial archives of Gisors were kept until the Revolution; before that it was a cellar. The lowest room of all, level with the bottom of the moat, was the real dungeon; light came only through narrow slits in the wall. The little light that filtered through these slits enabled two inmates of the room to carve strange bas-reliefs and various graffiti – the usual habit of prisoners – in the soft stone. Some date apparently from the fifteenth century, the others from 1575, a date that is carved in the stone together with the artist's initials. This may have been Nicholas Poulain, lieutenant to the provost of the police. As for the carvings, they may have been the work of a certain Jérémie

Bellanger, a fifteenth-century writer whose crimes are unknown. However, the prisoners carved scenes from the life of Christ, from the Last Supper to the suicide of Judas. But one can also make out a court ball, a hunting scene, two tourneys and the inscription: *Mater Dei memento mei*. This inscription is found also in the sculptures of the church of Gisors, together with various scenes carved on the walls; thus one clever archaeologist thought that the carvings were simply the work of the masons employed on the church in the sixteenth century and housed in the Prisoners' Tower. It sounds logical.

The fortress of Gisors played no great part during the Hundred Years' War. At first it was held by the King of France; Edward III vainly tried to conquer it in 1346. He could only burn part of the town. But after the defeat of Agincourt, the whole of Normandy was invaded. Gisors bravely held out for three weeks. In January 1419 the Duke of Clarence entered the castle and it was occupied by the English for thirty years. As early as 1446 brave La Hire attempted to retake the town; he failed and it was only in 1449 that Pierre de Brézé, Grand Seneschal of Normandy, recovered it. The English governor, Richard Merbury, was allowed full military honours and substantial grants of money. Brézé had preferred to negotiate instead of facing a long and costly siege.

After this Anglo-French rivalry, the history of the fortress seems to end. Royal agents were housed and assizes were held there. During the Wars of Religion armed troops passed through the city and spread terror, of which a diary, kept by a local citizen, is witness. Henri IV came several times to Gisors while fighting to conquer his capital. The royal apartments were completely destroyed, and more or less on the same spot the Duc de Penthièvre, the last lord of Gisors before the Revolution, built a covered market which was pulled down in 1920.

Lawns and a terrace decorated with flower-beds give a pleasant aspect to this part of the city. But one must follow first the long alley above the fortress moat. An archaeologist will find there the remains of the twelve towers which formerly flanked the ramparts. A visitor will admire the charming view of three valleys, hills and the rich apple orchards which give such charm to the Norman Vexin.

More than any other, the castle at Dourdan deserves to be called royal. Indeed, as early as the tenth century it was part of the estate of Hugues le Grand, Duke of France, so that it was not necessary to bring it into the royal estates. Hugues le Grand died in his castle at Dourdan (*apud castrum Dordinchum*) in July 966. Dourdan is well situated, on the margin of the huge forests where the kings used to hunt, in the middle of Hurepoix.

The castle of Dourdan is outstanding for two features especially. Firstly, it was completely rebuilt by Philippe-Auguste about 1222, benefiting by all that had been learned concerning military architecture from the castles of the

Orient. The towers were placed so that the besieged could enfilade, and there was not one part of the wall they could not protect. Besides, the keep, instead of standing in the middle of the fortress, as at Gisors and at most traditional fortresses of the Middle Ages, was erected at one corner of the perfect square made by the walls. It was thus the vital part of the fortifications.

Moreover, while Montlhéry, Etampes and Gisors are mere deserted ruins, Dourdan is still inhabited. Above the gateway, and on either side, where the town's salt stores once stood, the rooms have been converted into apartments.

Its history is similar to that of most fortresses: warriors fought, kings visited, men were imprisoned. Several noble ladies were prisoners there too, among them Philip the Fair's daughter-in-law, poor Jeanne de Bourgogne, who was imprisoned for several years after the famous scandal in which the King's three sons were involved. However, she was well revenged when her husband ascended the throne and came to fetch her in great array:

Before that, Blanche of Castille, St Louis' mother, had received Dourdan as her dowry. Then the castle was handed to Marguerite of Provence, the Saintly King's wife. Several charters point to the fact that Louis IX came several times to Dourdan, which he liked. So it is fully justified that in the keep built by his grandfather the King's bust – a replica of the one in the Sainte Chapelle – now welcomes the visitor.

Early in the fifteenth century Dourdan belonged to the Duc de Berry, Charles V's brother. This protector of arts and artists made his castle more comfortable and decorated it with collections of masterpieces. Dourdan is represented in the miniatures of the *Très riches heures du Duc de Berry*. Above a dense forest full of game and the green chessboard of the meadows, Philippe-Auguste's towers soar into the blue sky of the Ile-de-France.

Until then the Hundred Years War had practically spared Dourdan, but both town and castle were soon to feel its blows. Salisbury conquered them, and the royal banner of England floated over the tower where, after Joan of Arc had been captured, brave La Hire was imprisoned. The fief of Dourdan, at the end of the century, was entrusted by Louis XI to Admiral de Gravelle; he paid a heavy rent for it and repaired both church and castle. The annals of Dourdan testify to a number of passing shadows: Anne de Pisseleu, Francis I's mistress; Anne d'Este, the widow of the Duc de Guise. Huguenots and Catholics fought over it. Guise's son, Henri le Balafre, established his headquarters there, and set out in 1587 to defeat the Huguenots' German auxiliaries at Auneau. Dourdan then belonged to the League and closed its gates to Biron, who had been sent out by Henri IV to conquer the town in 1591. A man named Jacques Dargiens locked himself in the citadel and held out for three weeks, and Biron was victorious only by trickery. Captain Jacques left the fortress with arms and baggage, flying colours, beating drums, lighted slow-matches; the inhabitants felt relieved, and

the three following lines were engraved on the new church bell. They give a
fair picture of those unhappy days:

> *'La ville mise à sac, le feu en ce saint lieu,*
> *Maint bourgeois rançonné, à Dourdan priez Dieu*
> *Qu'à vous, à tout jamais, je les sonne meilleures.'*[1]

The days that followed were better, indeed. Louis XIII liked Dourdan. He
often came to hunt in the neighbouring forests; he even slept in the castle, where
he discussed the state of the kingdom with his trusty councillor, Baudru, the
governor of the city. He sent Anne of Austria there to recuperate after the birth
of Philippe, Louis XIV's brother. When Philippe was given the title and rank of
Monsieur, the King's brother, he received Dourdan as his fief. Down to
Philippe-Egalité, all his descendants bore the title of Lord of Dourdan.

Yet they hardly ever stayed in the castle. It housed the Dourdan authorities
and that is why Regnard went there. The author of *Le légataire universel* was in
charge of *Eaux et Forêts*, and he took this function very seriously, if we can
rely on the numerous deeds he examined. Taken over by the State during the
Revolution, the old castle became a prison. It was almost pulled down, but as
luck would have it, it was sold and saved.

Its present aspect is very different from that of the medieval tower in the
Très riches heures. As early as 1608, Sully filled the ditch which separated the
keep from the rest of its defences. A curtain wall replaced the Hôtel de Sancy,
where Louis XIII used to live. Recent excavations have brought to light the
remains of the old chapel of St John the Baptist, which was the castle oratory.
This has lately been acquired by the town of Dourdan.

'Often in the summer did the King go to the forest of Vincennes after having
heard mass, and he reclined against an oak tree and made us sit around him. And
those who had a law-suit came to speak to him, without hindrance from an
usher or any other such person.'

When, early in the fourteenth century, Joinville penned those lines which did
so much to make popular the image of a pious king administering justice under
an oak tree, the royal castle of Vincennes had belonged to the crown for over
three centuries. This is probably one of the characteristic features of Vincennes:
from Louis VII to Louis XVI, it never ceased to be the residence of the French
kings. It was the constant witness of dramas and notable events of such a kind
that at Vincennes we have a summary of the history of the nation.

That there was a forest at the gates of the capital was what first induced the

---

[1] The town sacked, and this holy place set on fire, and many citizens held to ransom; pray God
that at Dourdan I will bring better things for you evermore.

Capetians to build there a country house which was a fortress as well. Nothing remains of St Louis' manor or of the chapel he built to shelter a fragment of the Crown of Thorns. Notices fixed to the present military buildings simply mark the sites.

Yet we know that the kings used to stay in that woodland manor almost as often as in their palace at the Cité. Weddings were celebrated there, including in 1284 that of Philip the Fair and Jeanne of Navarre. Sumptuous festivities took place there; kings died (Louis the Quarrelsome in 1316, Charles the Fair in 1327), and people were tried there. In 1315, Enguerrand de Marigny was summoned before a court which was hostile to the power held by Philip the Fair's former superintendent of finances, and he left Vincennes for the gallows at Montfaucon.

Was it to erase the memory of evil or because St Louis' old *manerium* seemed too decrepit to Philippe of Valois that he decided to pull all the buildings down and gradually erect a really regal city. He died in 1350 before he was able to see his plan carried out and nothing but the big keep, which had been begun in 1337, showed above ground. Jean the Good, in spite of his setbacks when fighting against the English, continued the building up to the third story. Charles V, who had been born in Vincennes, hastened the building. It is generally agreed that the master-builder was Raymond du Temple, who also worked on the Louvre. The keep was completed in 1370.

In spite of many alterations, it is still an impressive pile of great majesty and power. Standing apart from the fortress, after the old Capetian tradition, it rises 200 feet above a moat nearly fifty feet deep. A square surrounding wall, crowned with crenellations above machiocolations, and provided with strong turrets at each of its four corners, constituted the first obstacle to any assailant. The keep proper, a big square tower with round towers at the angles, was five storeys high, crowned by a quadrangular building, the watch-tower, to which a polygonal staircase turret led. The halls, with pointed ceiling arches, resting on a central pillar, had few openings. Vincennes was a fortress, first and foremost.

Yet Charles V liked it. He looked upon it as a retreat, a residence to which he brought his library, his favourite treasure. Within those thick walls he felt secure. But the keep was not enough for him. He had a rectangular surrounding wall built nearly 1,300 yards in circumference, punctuated with nine high towers. Only one of these has kept its early aspect, the one which faced the village. It must be admitted that with its six storeys, its drawbridge and postern, it still has a forbidding aspect. The wise King had made no secret of his intentions. 'He had meant to turn the castle in the Forest of Vincennes into a closed city,' wrote Christine de Pisan, 'and there he meant to build fine manors for several lords, knights and others amongst those whom he loved best.'

This, basically, but for different reasons, was the idea behind Versailles, which Louis XIV was to bring to realization three centuries later.

The King's last work was the Sainte Chapelle, to replace the one built by St

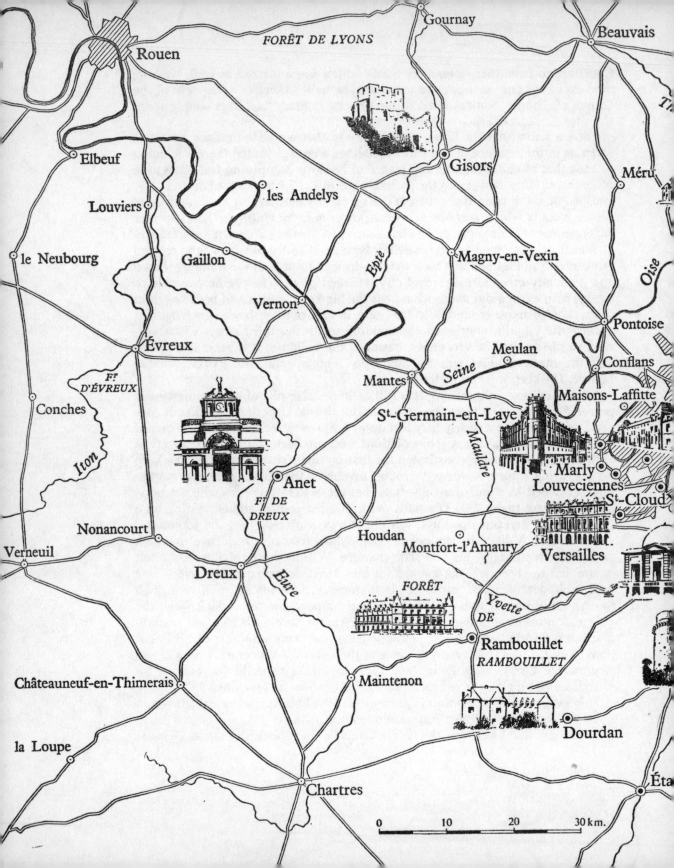

FORÊT DE LYONS

Gournay

Beauvais

Rouen

Elbeuf

les Andelys

Gisors

Méru

Louviers

Magny-en-Vexin

le Neubourg

Gaillon

Épte

Oise

Vernon

Pontoise

Évreux

Meulan

Conflans

Fᵗ D'ÉVREUX

Mantes

Seine

Maisons-Laffitte

Conches

Stᵗ-Germain-en-Laye

Marly

Louveciennes

Iton

Mauldre

Stᵗ-Cloud

Anet

Fᵗ DE DREUX

Nonancourt

Houdan

Montfort-l'Amaury

Versailles

Verneuil

Eure

FORÊT

Yvette DE

Dreux

Rambouillet

RAMBOUILLET

Châteauneuf-en-Thimerais

Maintenon

la Loupe

Dourdan

Chartres

Éta

0   10   20   30 km.

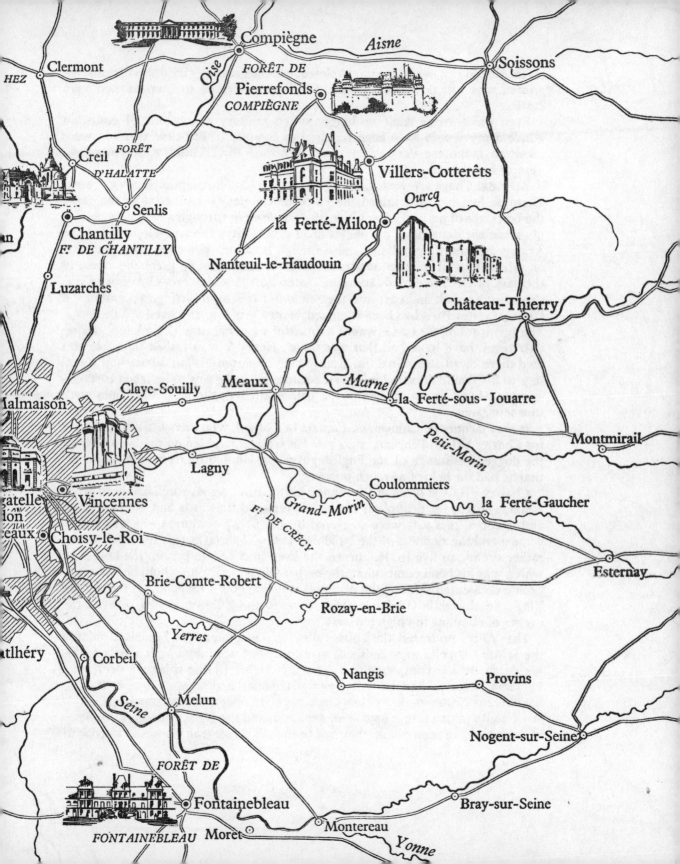

Compiègne

Aisne

Clermont

HEZ

FORÊT DE

Soissons

Oise

Pierrefonds

COMPIÈGNE

Creil

FORÊT

D'HALATTE

Villers-Cotterêts

Senlis

Ourcq

Chantilly

Fᵗ DE CHANTILLY

la Ferté-Milon

Luzarches

Nanteuil-le-Haudouin

Château-Thierry

Clayc-Souilly

Meaux

Murne

la Ferté-sous-Jouarre

Malmaison

Petit-Morin

Montmirail

Lagny

Coulommiers

la Ferté-Gaucher

gatelle
lon
eaux

Vincennes

Fᵗ DE CRÉCY

Grand-Morin

Choisy-le-Roi

Esternay

Brie-Comte-Robert

Rozay-en-Brie

Yerres

tlhéry

Corbeil

Nangis

Provins

Seine

Melun

Nogent-sur-Seine

FORÊT DE

Fontainebleau

Bray-sur-Seine

FONTAINEBLEAU

Moret

Montereau

Yonne

Louis. He did not live to see it completed, nor the growing city of his dreams: the ground was still devoid of houses. The lords preferred to keep to their own castles.

Even the fortress itself no longer suited military conditions. Of course, a whole army would have been required to conquer it. But new weapons were about to make the deep moats and the strong towers useless. Raymond du Temple had felt this.

At least, Charles V was able to give some splendid receptions at Vincennes. There he lavishly entertained the Emperor Charles IV and spent in the castle the best days of his life. After his death, France went through a very dark period: his successor's madness, his uncles' mad prodigality, the struggle between the Armagnacs and Burgundians, and a foreign invasion. Vincennes was the stage on which several momentous scenes were enacted, among them the arrest in the park of the Sire de Bois-Bourdon, Queen Isabella of Bavaria's lover, who was thrust into a sack and cast into the Seine. But it is more fitting to mention the fact that, after Paris had been occupied, Henry V of England lived at Vincennes. The furniture of the castle was in a dreadful state, because 'the soldiers, during two years, have looted all that was there'. Henry V refurnished the place and died there of an abdominal flu, after having imparted his last advice and warnings to his councillors and relatives. Because his body was to be taken to Westminster Abbey, it was boiled in the palace kitchen; the flesh and bones were thus separated.

It was Jacques de Chabannes, Captain of Corbeil, who reconquered the castle for Charles VII, on February 14, 1436. His troop scrambled up the keep, despite the dogged resistance of the English governor, Hunington. It is true, however, that he had the help of a French prisoner.

Charles VII lived often at Vincennes: his mistress, Agnès Sorel, had been given a house nearby, at Beauté-sur-Marne. He repaired the castle and the Florentine ambassadors, in 1461, were staggered by the park's resources – it was full of game – and the richness of the buildings. Louis XI thought that the fortress was rather dreary to live in. He turned the keep into a State prison, the keeper of which was his boon companion, the barber Olivier le Daim, whom he had made Comte de Meulan. Among the prisoners was François d'Alençon, set free by the King's death, while Olivier le Daim went to the gallows, having realized the danger of climbing too high too soon.

The Valois preferred the Loire valley to Vincennes. Yet Francis I ordered the Sainte Chapelle to be finished, as nothing had been done to it since Charles V's death. It was completed in 1552 under Henri III and solemnly dedicated. Philibert Delorme had built its ceiling, tribunes and treasure house. It is in flamboyant Gothic style, with a single nave, an apse and two small vestries. It fared badly in 1944. It is now being repaired, and the big stained-glass windows of the apse have been put in: they had been made after Jean Cousin's cartoons of the Revelation, and in spite of all that happened during the last century there are still many old fragments.

Charles IX, a great huntsman, often went to Vincennes. In the keep is the big room where he died on May 30, 1574, in terrible agony, haunted by the victims of the St Bartholomew massacre. Ronsard mourned the King in verse:

> Ah! malheureux cent fois, vieil chateau de Vincennes,
> Parc et bois malheureux, coupable de nos peines,
> En toy ce jeune prince a fermé ses beaux yeux. . . .[1]

The partisans of the League and the supporters of the King fought for the possession of Vincennes. Henry IV conquered it in 1594. He thought of having a more comfortable residence built there, a plan which appealed to Marie de Medici; but she was satisfied with a modest pavilion. Finally it was carried out by Mazarin. Then, in the southern part of the fortress, Le Vau erected the King's and the Queen's pavilions facing each other. The southern part of the walls was pierced with broad openings and, in the centre, the late Porte des Bois was turned into a gate, decorated on its inner face with a triumphal arch. The work, which had begun in 1653, was completed in 1660 when Louis XIV married Maria-Theresa and they spent their honeymoon there. The Cardinal had heaped his treasures in the castle, where he died on March 9, 1661. The King then did without a Prime Minister and shortly afterwards removed himself from Vincennes to Versailles.

Since the reign of Louis XIII the castle had been a state prison and prisoners were housed in the keep. The list of illustrious men who, during two centuries, were the King's guests in a way they had not desired is very long: princes of the blood, like Alexandre and César de Vendôme, Louis XIII's half-brothers, the Prince de Conti, the Grand Condé (during the Fronde), and Cardinal de Retz, who spent sixteen months there; ministers like Fouquet, carefully watched over by d'Artagnan; poisoners and witches like Mme Voisin or the Abbé Guibourg; pornographic writers like Crébillon the younger and the Marquis de Sade; dangerous thinkers or philosophers like Denis Diderot or Mirabeau; not forgetting the egregious Latude, a specialist in escapes.

Before he died Louis XIV suggested that his great-grandson should be taken to the King's Pavilion, which had not been lived in for the past forty-four years. Louis XV spent a few months there. Soon the Regent preferred to return to Paris and to the Palais-Royal.

During the eighteenth century Charles V's old castle had a varied fate. In the Devil's Tower a porcelain factory was established. The workmen, coming from Chantilly, were not very industrious. They spent most of their time in a local

---

[1] Old castle of Vincennes, oh! wretched park and forest, a hundred times accursed, you are guilty of our sorrow : here did this young prince close his fine eyes forever. . . .

tavern. Yet the King and the Marquise de Pompadour took some interest in the works, which were transferred to Sèvres in 1756. In the vacated buildings faience was then manufactured instead of porcelain. It was also in Vincennes that the pupils of the new military school were housed until Gabriel had finished his new building.

As a matter of fact Vincennes was of no great use. Louis XVI several times considered pulling it down. Three hundred thousand livres would have to be spent on it to put it in good repair, so its demolition was eventually decided upon in 1787. The three last prisoners (among whom was the Marquis de Sade) had been sent to the Bastille three years earlier. In spite of the protests of the last inmates, the fortress would have disappeared if the Revolution had not broken out. It saved the castle, which became a prison once more, while the keep was turned into a powder store.

It was a tragic prison. That the Duc d'Enghien was shot there on the night of March 19-20, 1804, is well known. Napoleon stained it with blood, and he turned it into a huge armoury, after having pulled down the towers. Imperial vandalism was not halted by the cost; so Vincennes, thanks to the Empire, had a few more illustrious guests – the two Polignacs, the banker Ouvrard, the cardinals and bishops who had been courageous enough to stand up to the Emperor's tyranny after the Pope had been arrested.

Daumesnil, who commanded the citadel in 1814, refused to surrender it and threatened to blow it up. After the Hundred Days he held out longer still. Then Vincennes surrendered to the army.

Throughout the nineteenth century the military ruined the old apartments, erected hideous buildings inside the walls, filled the inner courtyards with cumbersome barracks, while the ramparts were turned into a secondary fortress with casemates. The remains of Louis IX's palace suffered wanton destruction. Le Vau's buildings were pulled down. The Sainte Chapelle was cut in two by a wooden floor and it was even thought to pull it down. A part of the keep was used as a storeroom for weapons.

Yet, Vincennes still served as a prison. Barbes, Raspail, Berryer and Odilon Barrot (the two last following the *coup d'état* of December 2, 1851) came there. After the Commune, which occupied the fort for a short while, the army came back and methodically continued its destructive activities.

A well-organized campaign, between the two world wars, succeeded in getting Vincennes restored to the Department for Historical Monuments. The War Museum was organized in the Queen's pavilion, but the army returned at the beginning of the Second World War. The German troops stayed there for four years. In 1944 they shot thirty hostages there. An explosion destroyed the King's Pavilion, and a fire destroyed part of the Queen's Pavilion, but now, with skill and taste, the official architects are endeavouring to heal the wounds and restore Vincenne's former appearance. Much has already been done. The Sainte

Chapelle, the keep, and the two pavilions have been restored. Le Vau's arcades and triumphal arch have been freed. When the military buildings and modern barracks and the casemates, which have neither defensive value nor use, are pulled down, the capital will have regained one of its noblest royal castles.

At the border between Valois and Picardy, the castle of La Ferté-Milon arose chronologically between Vincennes, the work of Charles V, and Pierrefonds. At La Ferté-Milon, as at Pierrefonds, which came a little later, we find once again the hand of Charles' younger son, Louis of Orléans, who had married the charming Valentina Visconti. Ferocious family feuds were raging between the mad King's uncles and their nephew, and he was obliged to look for powerful protection. Indeed, it was a far cry from the little blockhouse (ferté), erected by Milon on a mound above the city, and the vast and powerful fortress that Louis' architects began to build in 1393.

Its history is short. It was a royal abode for only a brief period. For several centuries it had been one of the most envied properties of the counts of Flanders, after having belonged to those of Vermandois. Then it became part of the French royal estate. The fortress was in a rather ruinous state, but it was a good stronghold at one corner of the estate. By the end of the fourteenth century Charles VI entrusted it to his brother, who had it completely rebuilt, overlooking a vast expanse of forests, rivers and rich peaceful meadows.

The plan was grandiose. The rectangular keep stands at the tip of the promontory above the city. It continues in a high façade, flanked with three big towers, two of which stand on either side of a majestic gate. The walls are topped by the sculpted corbels of old machicolations, pierced with a triple line of rectangular mullion windows.

It is an impressive fortress, thanks to its dimensions and thick walls, now breached; but a new style of architecture can nevertheless be detected. Louis of Orléans, who liked the arts and artists, sought to combine his own tastes with the necessities of defence. There was a sentry road on the wall and machicolations, but the windows were wide and open to the light and the sun. There were archery ranges, and the drawbridge was as well protected as in the thirteenth century, but above it a beautiful bas-relief was set in an ornamented frame, the sides of which are decorated with trefoils. It was not a war-like scene which had been sculpted above the entrance, but one of the most touching and graceful episodes in the life of the Virgin: her crowning. Other sculptures embellish the three towers and the keep. Sensitive – too sensitive – to feminine charms, Louis had statues ordered which were not of warriors but of women, heroic and serious, of which the heads have unfortunately been broken.

Thus, amidst such powerful defensive elements, appeared a concern for decoration which from then on was never absent. We shall never know what the finished castle would have looked like. The only façade to be completed was the east one, and on November 23, 1407, while returning from the Hôtel Barbette, where he had been visiting Queen Isabella of Bavaria, Louis of Orléans was treacherously murdered at the instigation of the Duke of Burgundy. The stones which had already been cut on the western front were never used.

Thenceforth, the usual story followed: the castle was used by the supporters of the League while Henri IV was striving to reconquer his kingdom. Antoine de Sainte-Chamons held it for over four years. As soon as he had won, the King had the defences dismantled. The fortress played its last part at the time of the Fronde in 1652.

This impressive ruin would be of no interest except to archaeologists, but for the idea that it may have been for several years before the eyes of the son of a burgher of La Ferté-Milon, a little orphan brought up by his grandmother: Jean Racine. His grandmother Desmoulins' house, his uncle Sconin's house, and the old mansion where Jean de la Fontaine married his beautiful cousin Marie Héricart, are landmarks which give the little Valois town possibly more charm and interest than do the headless statues and the heavy walls of Louis of Orléans' fortress.

We meet the same prince again at Pierrefonds. This famous castle, which occupies an extremely strong position above the little lake formed by the Berne, on the edge of the forest of Compiègne, was completely rebuilt by him at the end of the fourteenth century. It replaced an older citadel, built on the same site by the lords of Nivelon in the early middle ages. Its situation was essential to the security of monarchy, and the forest of Compiègne was a great attraction to the hunting kings of France. Philippe-Auguste acquired the castle and its rights in 1181. Two centuries later, in 1392, Charles VI handed the whole Valois to his brother Louis. The latter entrusted the master builder of Senlis, a certain Jean le Noir, with the task of rebuilding the castle, which wars and the years had brought into disrepair. Le Noir set to work on it, and before 1407, when the Prince was murdered by the Duke of Burgundy, Pierrefonds had been completed.

Thenceforth its story is of nothing but long decay. After the death of Louis of Orléans, the king of France took the castle back. He handed it over to the care of the Comte de Saint-Pol, who set fire to it when he had to evacuate it in 1413. Charles of Orlèans, the son of Louis and Valentina Visconti, a delightful poet, was captured by the English at Agincourt. To while away his long captivity he wrote tender but melancholy poems. The English occupied the castle and were dislodged only after thirty years, at the end of the Hundred Years War.

Pierrefonds returned to the royal estate and its story was like that of all other fortresses. It was fought over at the time of the League. It was conquered by the Lord of Rieux in 1591. Epernon and Marshal de Biron vainly tried to drive him out. Finally, Rieux was taken and hanged two years later. Henri IV gave the castle to Antoine d'Estrées, father of his mistress Gabrielle. Antoine's son,

François, was silly enough to conspire against Louis XIII in 1616, for which he was punished. Pierrefonds paid for its master's impudence; the fortress was entirely dismantled.

It was just a magnificent ruin when Napoleon I – no one knows why – bought it for 2,950 francs. His nephew, Napoleon III, was passionately fond of archaeology, and when he became Emperor he gave Viollet-le-Duc the task of restoring the crumbling walls.

Archaeologists are usually rather hard on this celebrated architect. It is obvious that at Pierrefonds Viollet-le-Duc rebuilt Louis d'Orléans citadel after old engravings, the accuracy of which is very doubtful. He completely improvised where nothing was left and was not always successful. 'The rebuilding of the apartments is but a long-drawn-out blunder,' stated Raymond Ritter without mincing words. One can say the same about the exterior fortifications, which are nothing if not childish, the south front almost wholly modern, to say nothing of the west front with the huge but obviously false Alexander Tower. What part of it is authentic? The north-north-east front with its three towers, named Hector, Josué and Godefroy. Their condition was not too bad when Viollet-le-Duc started operations in 1857, and they are large enough to display the beauty of Pierrefonds and its importance in the history of French military architecture.

The chief characteristic of the three towers are their powerful defences. Their builders had realized that a continuous line of defence had to be organized, enabling the besieged to get quickly and safely to all threatened points.

Curtains and towers have two castellated storeys, the top floor of the curtains being on a level with the lower battlements of the towers. Thus was organized the horizontal line that was sought by the builders.

As for the rest of the castle, it is well worth a visit. The drawbridge, the fort at the entrance, the grand inner façade with its sculpted gallery, even the chapel: everything was invented by Viollet-le-Duc. But the chapel itself is a success; on one of its piers the architect himself was portrayed as St James Major. The keep has been much altered and it is obvious that neither the Emperor's nor the Empress Eugenie's study have much in common with the earlier parts of the building. The Empress' ladies-in-waiting sat for the portraits of the heroines in the Great Hall.

And yet, when night falls, and the towers and ramparts of Pierrefonds stand out against the sky as on some romantic lithograph, we can forgive Viollet-le-Duc, because his castle shows us something of the beauty and grandeur of medieval fortresses in the days when they were young and powerful.

CHAPTER II

CHATEAUX AND MANOR HOUSES
OF THE RENAISSANCE

THERE is no break in the continuity either of history or architecture, and the breaks we insert, though useful, are wholly artificial. Of course, they correspond to trends and tendencies, but one must be careful not to be too positive in seeking support from the reality of dates and events.

It is generally accepted that the wars in Italy marked a turning point in the chateau architecture of France: from over the Alps the French kings brought back, besides the artists, a new taste for luxury, elegance and beauty. Fortresses were no longer useful and were superseded by pleasant, richly-decorated residences; the moats and the talus that flanked the ramparts disappeared and were replaced by tastefully ornamented parks and gardens. It is not untrue to say that there were in fact two Renaissances. The first took place shortly before the period of Francis I, and its effects are noticeable in the royal chateaux at Meudon, Villers-Cotterêts and especially Fontainebleau.

These chateaux were of the early Renaissance, and distinctly influenced by the ornamented Italian style, which took the place of the Gothic style after the end of the fifteenth century. Yet they did not belong entirely to the Renaissance. Meudon, for instance, had been built in 1520; the Duchesse d'Etampes, Francis I's mistress, embellished it in 1540 and the Cardinal of Lorraine completely changed it in accordance with the taste of the second and classical Renaissance between 1552 and 1560. Moreover, the terrace and gardens date from the second half of the seventeenth century and the Grand Dauphin, Louis XIV's son, had the new chateau built between 1706 and 1709.

As for Fontainebleau, the fact that this wonderful palace belongs to the Renaissance can be accepted, though there was already a medieval fortress there at the time of St Louis. It is well known that Francis I considerably enlarged the chateau, which he actually created. Yet all his Valois successors left their mark there and its exterior was altered several times under Louis XV and Napoleon I. Nevertheless, Fontainebleau is inseparable from the style typical of Francis I's reign. The same comment could apply to St Germain-en-Laye, though it is less varied in style than Fontainebleau; it owes its unity to the destruction of Henri

II's chateau. The same applies to many other buildings, whether royal or not.

It would seem fairly coherent, however, to write about each chateau from its earliest construction: Fontainebleau, St Germain-en-Laye and Meudon. They all belonged to the Renaissance. Then we shall follow the history of each and the changes in their layout through the centuries, besides the changes in style brought by changes in taste.

Fontainebleau is not the oldest of the chateaux built under Francis I's influence; it is likely that Meudon or Villers-Cotterêts are older. But Meudon no longer exists and Villers-Cotterêts is not very important. Fontainebleau, on the contrary, and thanks to its size and its style, has left its mark on Renaissance art. There was a school of Fontainebleau, the tenets of which were followed by many artists in building the famous chateaux on the Loire. It therefore seems fair and logical to begin with this palace, called by Napoleon 'a true kingly residence, a house surviving for centuries'.

The historians all agree that Fontainebleau owes its birth to the proximity of the large forest, full of game, and to the existence of Bliaud, one of the few springs in the forest at which huntsmen could water their horses. But nothing remains of the feudal castle built before St Louis except a big square keep, the door and windows of which were rebuilt in the sixteenth century. It is now surrounded by other parts of the chateau and is named after the saintly king who came to Fontainebleau on several occasions. What surrounds the Porte Dorée, around the Cour Ovale, was built upon the old foundations.

The one who is wholly responsible for the chateau is Francis I. As soon as he returned from captivity in Spain in 1528 he undertook the restoration of what was left and started building new parts. It seems that there never was a general plan: wings or pavilions were added individually according to the kings' tastes or needs.

The master builder was Gilles Le Breton. He built the wings of the Cour du Cheval-Blanc (or Cour des Adieux) which he connected by a gallery to the Cour Ovale, the aspect and decoration of which he completely altered. Pointed roofs, and bricks underlining the windows, were among the details which displayed a new style, quite distinct from medieval architecture. Gilles Le Breton was remarkable for the simplicity of his new devices and for the classical elegance of his inventions.

The main characteristic of architecture under Francis I is the originality of the interior decoration. It lies at the origin of the school which has taken the name of the chateau. It was created by two Italian masters: Il Rosso, known as Maître Rous, and Primaticcio. Maître Rous, who started work at the chateau in 1530, decorated the Francis I Gallery with stucco-framed panels, intimately blending painting and sculpture. Here the new element in his artistic ideas was to be found; yet it was not so very new, having been associated with the style of older French diptyches. As early as the twelfth century, at St Aubin d'Angers, an unknown master was blending sculpture and frescoes in the higher parts of the cloister arcades. Rosso's constant use of that process in the Fontainebleau gallery is the secret of its radiant beauty. It is a pity that some crude restoration under Louis-Philippe deprived the paintings of some of their quality, but we still have the delightful sculptures, the whiteness of which glistens round the paintings: beautiful and dignified statues of men and women, chubby angels and playful babies. René Boyvin's engravings reveal what the sculptured frames were like when new.

Maître Rouse worked at this until his death in 1541. Primaticcio had worked with him for ten years. He had been put in charge of the work (as was Le Brun at Versailles), and supervised the creation of the bronze statues in the gardens as well as the work on the tapestries that were eventually hung in the galleries. It is a great pity that most of his work has been destroyed. A fireplace in the Queen's drawing-room, the decoration of the Duchesse d'Etampes' room, which was left untouched by Gabriel when he built the Escalier du Roi, still enable us to admire his talent and to regret the destruction of the Galerie d'Ulysse, which ran along the southern wing of the Cour du Cheval Blanc, where the Louis XV wing was built. All that is left – long, slender naked women with small, high breasts – inspired all the artists who belonged to the Fontainebleau School.

Francis I's death did not stop the work on the chateau. In the south wing of the Cour Ovale Henri II built the gallery which has been given his name and which was in fact the ballroom. Le Breton began it, but Philibert Delorme came soon after and changed the planned vaulted ceiling into a partitioned one. Primaticcio undertook the decoration. Assisted by Nicolo de l'Abbate, by the carpenters Francisco Scibec and Carpi, he carried out the eight great mythological groups which decorate the space between the ceiling and the ten windows of the hall. The recesses were decorated with similar frescoes. The whole ballroom is gorgeously beautiful: embellished by the graceful Diane de Poitiers for whom it was conceived, despite nineteenth century restoration, it still dazzles the eyes.

Philibert Delorme did not stop there. He also built the Horseshoe Staircase (changed into something quite different in 1634), the gallery in the upper chapel, the terrace in front of Francis I's gallery and other buildings which have disappeared. After Henri II's death, Philibert Delorme had to resign and Primaticcio took charge, having been appointed Supervisor of Buildings by Catherine de Medici. During the last part of his life he built the wing of the 'Fine Fireplace' (or 'de l'Ancienne Comédie'), overlooking the Cour de la Fontaine. With its open-air staircase, its Doric pilasters and high-pointed roofs, it has a wholly Italian aspect. After Primaticcio's death in 1570, Jean Bulland built the wing alongside Diane's garden which duplicates the Queen's apartment.

At Fontainebleau each king sought to add something to what had gone before, which explains the lack of unity. Henri IV created the buildings round the kitchens and pantries courtyard. They are well built, in a simple, dignified style, in white stone with high-pointed roofs. They have a slightly rural aspect. In his reign the canopy above the gate into the Cour Ovale, devised by Primaticcio, was built. Louis XIII was christened under that monumental gate. It is now called the Font, though it should properly be known as the Dauphin Gate. In the east wing of the Cour de la Fontaine Jacques Mathieu erected for the King a huge fireplace which was dismantled in 1775. What is left of it, together with a bas-relief of Henri IV on horseback, can be seen now in the so-called Saint Louis Room.

The chateau was never completed. Louis XIII merely saw that Philibert Delorme's horseshoe staircase was replaced by Jean Ducerceau's, the one we see now in the Cour des Adieux. It is quite wrong still to refer to it as the Horseshoe; its shape is quite different. In the wing next to the old keep, opening upon the Cour Ovale, Louis XIII was born in the Louis XIII drawing-room. The walls and ceilings are decorated with mythological subjects. Mythology was used throughout the Palace of Fontainebleau, and from Francis I to Louis XIV painters and sculptors went to it for inspiration, putting under the prince's eyes a glorious rendering of the lessons they had been taught, though today the story of Theagene and Chariclea, painted by Ambroise Dubois in the King's room, is a little obscure. The Holy Trinity Chapel was built by Francis I, having been begun in 1608, and decorated by Louis XIII.

It would be wrong to think that Fontainebleau was deserted under Louis XIV. Of course, the Sun-King was mostly interested in Versailles, but he and his court came often to Fontainebleau, and there he housed foreign princes who visited him during his reign; in 1657, Christina of Sweden had her former lover, Monadelschi, murdered in the Galerie des Cerfs because she had had enough of him. Sentimental visitors are shown the Grand Ecuyer's mail shirt, which thwarted the daggers of the Queen's executioners.

The alterations effected by Louis XIV, Louis XV and Louis XVI were mostly concerned with the interior of the chateau. Mme de Maintenon's apartments are on the first floor, above the Porte Dorée. The King's study, which had become the Council Room, was gorgeously decorated by Bouchier, who painted the ceiling; also by Van Loo and J. B. Pierre, who did the walls. The decoration of Marie-Antoinette's apartments, which open upon Diana's gardens, remind us of those which Mique and the brothers Rousseau devised for the Petit Trianon. Was it really necessary in Louis XV's reign to have Gabriel pull down the south wing of the Cour du Cheval-Blanc, destroy the wonderful Galerie d'Ullysse, and replace it by a dull building like the one that bears his name at Versailles?

Gabriel's destructive activity was continued during Napoleon's reign. The Emperor blotted out the west wing: he turned the Cour du Cheval-Blanc into a main courtyard, pulled down the wing that shut it in and had a railing erected instead. That courtyard framed one of the most moving scenes of Napoleon's reign: his farewell to his soldiers after his abdication on April 20, 1814.

The Emperor left a deep mark upon the chateau. Recollections of the various kings, or of the beautiful ladies who ruled there from Diane de Poitiers to Marie Antoinette, fade before those of the Corporal. The rooms in which he lived have been accurately recreated: below Francis I's gallery, in the wing erected in the time of Louis XV, are his study, the map room with the large tables over which he leaned to look at them, the desk he took along with him during his campaigns, and, on the first floor, in his State Apartments, the famous little hat.

Several of the principal episodes of Napoleon's reign took place at Fontaine-bleau. One thinks of his struggle with Pius VII when visiting the rooms where the Pope was imprisoned; of Josephine and the King of Rome, when looking at the empress's tapestry frame, or at the little ship with which Marie-Louise's son once played. Fontainebleau owes almost as much to the emperor as to Francis I. As for Louis-Philippe and Napoleon III, it would be unfair to make them responsible for the restorations which have stripped both Francis I's Gallery and the Ballroom of some of their beauty. The painters who wrecked Fontainebleau were men of poor talent. One must give the sovereigns credit for having looked after the palace. They were the victims of the taste of the period, which was bad.

Fontainebleau's finest decoration is the forest which surrounds both chateau and town. Yet the gardens that were designed and embellished by the inmates of the palace should not be ignored. Francis I liked those 'delightful deserts' and had a garden made south of the Cour du Cheval-Blanc. The beautiful Pine Cave, close beside the chateau, is a grotto decorated by four figures of Atlas who display their powerful muscles. The style of Serlio can be recognized. It was Francis, too, who had the Carp Pond excavated and its fine fishes very much admired as early as the seventeenth century. In the middle of the pond, and almost as if suspended between heaven and earth, there is a tiny island on which a little pavilion stands. It has often been repaired and Napoleon himself did his bit; it was during the Empire that the classical gardens planned by Francis I were turned into 'English' gardens and planted with many exotic trees, like cypress or tulip trees from Louisana, which gave the formal French parks a completely new look.

The classical aspect is still present, however, on the other side of the pond, with a fine Le Notre flower-garden. It was first planted during Henri IV's reign, but its four symmetrical tree-clusters at the four corners of a square pond have a straight and geometrical aspect that is characteristic of the Versailles gardens. In former days the basin was decorated with a statue of the Tiber. Henri IV had the Grand Canal dug, too, a quarter of a league in length on the axis of the centre bed. It ended in the waterfall basin, built by Louis XIV and decorated with mythological statues. Alas! the water dried up long ago, and the waterfalls have been destroyed.

Henri IV's park beyond the Grand Canal, which was completed during his grandson's reign, is now rather abandoned; its symmetrical shaded walks remind us of the classical period. The maze is there and the King's Vine too; its tasty grape is much sought after by connoisseurs.

Lastly, beside the Holy Trinity chapel, between Napoleon's rooms and Marie-Antoinette's, lies Diana's Garden. Ducerceau planned it in 1579 and it has been successively known as the Box Garden, the Aviary Garden, and the Queen's Garden, but was finally given the name of the goddess whose statue, cast by the Kellers in 1684, stands there.

Such are the parks and gardens, a little ill-matched like the palace buildings themselves. The sovereigns who lived at Fontainebleau found more pleasure and rest in them than at Versailles. It has been rightly observed that the English Garden, with its winding paths, its vistas always opening on the famous Fontaine Belle Eau, and its rare trees, reminded Napoleon of the charms of Malmaison. It was perhaps for its peaceful simplicity that the Emperor preferred Fontainebleau to all other chateaux.

The main work at Fontainebleau was begun in 1528. Work at Meudon had been started a few years earlier, but there is nothing to reveal its earlier aspect apart from a few old prints; yet the history of that royal residence is fairly well known.

In the early Middle Ages there was already a castle at Meudon, 'the yellow-earth hill'. Until the beginning of the fifteenth century it belonged to the family which bore that name, and in 1415 it passed to a Lucca money-lender, named Ysbarre, who had settled in Paris. Eleven years later his associate, Guillaume Sanguin, bought the castle from him, and it remained in the family for more than a century. In 1527 Antoine Sanguin, who had taken holy orders and later became a cardinal, pulled down the old castle and built a new and very modern one which he gave to his niece, Anne de Pisseleu, 'so that she could honourably find a husband': a rather pious wish, as that lovely girl became Francis I's mistress. Anne completed the chateau with two pavilions at right-angles to the main front and had the first park planned. Her lover often visited her there.

When she married Jean de la Brosse she took the title of Duchesse d'Etampes. She left the Court when Francis I died, and sold Meudon to the Archbishop of Rheims, the Cardinal of Lorraine, in 1552. Using plans drawn up by Primaticcio, and with the help of Nicolo de l'Abbate, Barbiere, Trébati or Jean le Roux, the Cardinal built his celebrated grotto, separated from the pavilions by a double staircase. The grotto was decorated with sculptured fauns; Ronsard praised it in one of his poems and one of the pavilions was named after him in consequence. The Cardinal of Lorraine also built two hot-houses for orange trees, the one above the other (they have survived) and the first walls to support the terrace from which Ronsard used to survey Paris.

Meudon remained in the Cardinal's family until 1654. Henri of Navarre was there when he heard of the murder of his cousin Henri III at St Cloud. The chateau was inhabited for a long time by Marguerite of Lorraine, who had married Gaston of Orleans. It was eventually sold in 1654 to Abel Servien, Superintendent of Finance. This great servant of the State, who had signed the Peace of Westphalia, undertook to repair it once more. Le Vau altered the central pavilion by building high attics above it. The terrace was completed and strengthened by buttresses. The beds in front of the grotto were altered and other ornamental beds were planted. The estate grew larger. When he died Abel Servien, who had spent his whole fortune on his enterprises, was in debt to the extent of 1,600,000 livres.

His son, the Marquis de Sablé, sold Meudon to Louvois, who entrusted Mansart with reconstructing the interior. Van der Meulen painted the long gallery, and Monnoyer decorated it with lovely piers. Above all, Louvois had the park reconstructed. By the skilful purchase of land he enlarged his estate considerably. Then Le Nôtre planned the wonderful vista which, in the axis of the terrace, opens upon a landscape of trees and ponds. Water was brought through large pipes and enlivened the gardens with numerous waterfalls and fountains which delighted visitors. Instead of the old parterre, new gardens were designed that looked like embroidered floral bands, studded with yew trees. In the higher as well as the lower gardens, clusters of trees and basins were planted or built. Alleys intersected, opening vistas through the woods. In the end Le Nôtre quarrelled with Louvois, who got Mansart back to carry out his task. Three years later Louvois died, more or less in disgrace, and his widow was only too happy to exchange this expensive estate for Choisy, which the king had offered her. Louis XIV was planning to give Meudon to his son, the Grand Dauphin.

'I have been hoping for a long time that you would acquire Meudon,' Le Nôtre told the King. 'I am glad it is yours, but I would be sorry if you had acquired it earlier: it would not have been so beautiful.' Louis XIV supervised the work himself. He was passionately fond of garden planning.

New statues were brought to Meudon, together with a geographical globe, resembling the one installed at Marly: it had been brought over from Versailles. In the lower garden the Chestnut Tree Hall became the Hall of Cleopatra. New basins and fountains were built or dug. The park was further enlarged by adding to it that of Chaville, which the King bought in 1698 from Louvois' mother, the 'Lady Chancellor' Le Tellier.

Louis XIV supervised the planting of the flowers: tulips, white lilies, narcissi, gilly-flowers 'for Monseigneur's gardens', and just as he had at Versailles decided upon the right way to visit the gardens, so in 1701 he did the same for Meudon:

'One should arrive by way of the avenue, and afterwards reach the courtyard, there one must leave the carriage, by way of the superb terrace.' The care he bestowed upon the embellishment of Meudon did not prevent him from saving what money he could and from seeing that it was not wasted. The interior of the chateau was hung with curtains that had already been used at Versailles.

The Grand Dauphin liked Meudon. He was a strange man, rather unpredictable and clumsy, according to the Palatine Princess, who did not like him. To the chateau he brought his mistress, Mlle Choin, whom he probably later secretly married, just as his father had married Mme de Maintenon. At Meudon the Grand Dauphin could easily indulge in his favourite pastime of hunting. He had the Chestnut Wing added to the structure, and he gave Jouvenet, Audran and Coypel the task of altering the interior by creating private apartments. In 1702 he had a chapel built.

Thanks to Louis XIV's stubbornness, his grandson, the Grand Dauphin's son, had become King of Spain. As the sovereign was ageing, more courtiers were gathering round the heir to the throne and, in spite of enlargements, Meudon was again too small. It was then decided to build the new chateau, which Hardouin-Mansart carried out between 1706 and 1709. It was a difficult period and the Spanish war was bleeding France white. The new chateau was built in accordance with the austerity of the times: it was pleasant, well-proportioned and sober simultaneously. The Grand Dauphin did not enjoy it for long: he died of smallpox on April 14, 1711. In the apartments of his daughter-in-law, the Duchess of Burgundy, his furniture and jewels were auctioned. Though the estate was still a royal residence, it was no longer in constant use. Czar Peter the Great visited it in May 1717. The Duchesse de Berry, Louis XV's aunt, lived there for some time with her lover, the Comte de Riom, Lauzun's nephew. During Louis XV's reign it was used only as a hunting lodge. A night fête was organized there for the Dauphin in 1735, and yet another Dauphin, Louis XVI's elder son, died there a few days after the meeting of the States-General in 1789.

The Convention brought the chemist Berthollet to Meudon (he was supervisor of artillery experiments), together with a general better known for a novel than for his military achievements, Choderlos de Laclos. The author of *Les Liaisons Dangereuses* and the chemist began the ruin of this beautiful chateau, a task which was pursued thoroughly throughout the next century. The Old Chateau was turned into workshops, and the orangery into a balloon factory. Finally, a fire broke out in the Old Chateau. In 1803 Napoleon had its remains pulled down and that was the end of the beautiful Renaissance chateau, except for a few columns which were carried to Paris.

The New Chateau was repaired and the gardens redecorated. In 1811 Meudon became the residence of the little King of Rome and his Empress, but it was devastated by the Prussians in 1814 and 1815. Various exalted people lived there during the nineteenth century, from Don Pedro of Portugal[1] to Jérôme Bonaparte, Napoleon III's cousin, better known as Plon-plon.[2]

In January 1871 the Prussians bombarded Paris from the terrace at Meudon, and the chateau caught fire on January 31st. After the fire it was in a sad condition and remained thus for several years. The State did not care for a chateau which was merely a reminder of régimes that had been destroyed. It was eventually given to the astronomer Janssen. He built an observatory there; but first of all, out of sheer hatred for the monarchy, he savagely mutilated what was left of the chateau – the wings were razed to the level of the ground floor and the central building was topped with a hideous dome: it would have been difficult to do more damage. It is now hard to imagine how the building once looked. Janssen's successors jealously barred access to what was left, the Renaissance orangery and the garden. The remains were distributed far and wide. An aviation park and the Air Museum surround the Chalais Pond. The Institut de Chimie Végétable is somewhere else. The Ministry of Fine Arts patiently tries to restore the former estate and has already succeeded in recovering the Chalais Pond.

We can only hope that one day the park will recover its former beauty. Happily, the forest is still there, where Parisians in search of fresh air gather lily of the valley early in the spring; so is the terrace whence one may gaze at the landscape of stone and trees which enraptured Ronsard in the sixteenth century: '*De là tu verras Paris la grandville*'.

The forest of Retz – the name once given to the huge expanse round the little town of Villers Cots de Retz – saw the birth of a chateau that is far too neglected by travellers. It is also a chateau of major artistic interest, since its Renaissance decorations are set in a framework from which modern shapes shyly try to emerge.

A medieval citadel stood there, which belonged to the Comtes de Valois, and was set on fire by the English in 1429. For more than a century the castle was deserted. When he became king, Francis I resolved to have it rebuilt, keeping its general design: two rectangular courtyards, one behind the other and of unequal sizes, surrounded by buildings. He also kept part of the outer walls of the former manor, built round the smaller courtyard. Those walls were flanked by pavilions, and between the two courts a central building was erected, the 'King's Lodgings', according to Androuet du Cerceau's drawing.

Guillaume and Jacques Le Breton, brothers most likely, or cousins of Gilles Le Breton, who was also working at that time at Fontainebleau, were the master-builders. In seventeen years the King spent 202,907 livres, 5 sous, 5 deniers on Villers-Cotterêts: a huge sum of money, which shows how much the King cared

[1] The last Emperor of Brazil.
[2] The son of Jérôme Bonaparte, Napoleon's brother, King of Westphalia.

for the place. He moved into it as easily as 1535 and he came quite often. In 1539 he signed there the famous ordinance of Villers-Cotterêts. Prepared by Guillaume Poyet, it was a regular code of legal procedure, one of the consequences of which was to introduce marriages.

Henri II was less interested in Villers-Cotterêts. Yet he built a pavilion in the south-west corner, the quiet architecture of which is in contrast with the grandeur of the King's Lodgings. Philibert Delorme had already been in charge of the works for several years. He was responsible in 1555 for a fountain, which later disappeared, like his lovely chapel in the park, built more or less after the design of Anet; a drawing of it remains.

Villers-Cotterêts experienced changing fortunes. During the wars, Catherine de Medici merely ordered Primaticcio to surround the chateau with a moat, but this was not done. It was left uncared for, and Androuet du Cerceau bewailed its condition. Henri IV had some slight repairs carried out, and Louis XIV got Le Nôtre to plan the park and the gardens. Because the chateau is so very close to the forest, such expenses had been thought unnecessary until then. East of the chateau there was nothing but bowers planted to form squares, and on the west a few flower beds and an orchard. Le Nôtre altered the whole with his usual taste. In the eighteenth century the chateau passed to the Orleans: Philippe-Joseph, who was known later as Philippe-Egalité, entertained there lavishly and hunted in the forest. He also altered the chateau but not for the better.

Villers-Cotterêts was spared during the Revolution. In 1808 an Imperial decree turned it into a workhouse. The windows were walled up and false ceilings were built. The whole interior was changed. Today it is an asylum for the aged of the Seine department.

In spite of such a fate, the façade of the King's Lodgings still smiles at visitors as it did in the time of Francis I. It is a picture of charm and refinement. The whole of Renaissance art blossoms there delightfully. Is it purely Italian, or does it borrow something from France? Historians disagree. It is obvious that the master-builders took their inspiration from the gateway of the Cour Ovale at Fontainebleau. But the new styles were interpreted with great liberty. On the first floor there is a loggia, at the back of which were twin bays; it reminds us of similar loggias at Blois, built under Louis XII. The whole front is decorated with chubby Cupids, shells and salamanders, Francis I's heraldic beast, all of them rather mannered. It is a pity that the tops of the buildings were so badly altered in the eighteenth century. The balustrade above the cornice has disappeared and the dormer-windows have been simplified.

Inside, the so-called State Hall is actually the old chapel and it is quite possible that the diptych at the back, dated 1539, was originally placed there. The hall is vaulted, but an intermediary ceiling conceals the vaulting, and the bays which had opened upon the original courtyard have been filled up. Between those which are still open elegantly shaped columns still exist, decorated with royal emblems. Two straight staircases with coffered ceilings lead up to the hall. The largest is decorated with rosettes and salamanders, and is a forerunner of the one in the Louvre. The other has been decorated with wonderful high-reliefs of charming mythological scenes: a buxom Venus allowing a satyr to fondle her, and, a little further away, punishing a weeping Cupid. Hercules fights the Nemean lion, and Apollo fights Marsyas. Mythology provided Renaissance artists with an inexhaustible supply of themes.

The other buildings round the courtyard were handled much more simply: dormer-windows in brick decorated with fireballs. This was all completed under Francis I, as evidenced by the King's initial on the chimneys. As for the little courtyard, it was turned into a tennis-court.

Such was the charm of Villers-Cotterêts: it was less a castle than a manor house, a building conceived on a human level. Contrary to Fontainebleau or St Germain-en-Laye, it kept within modest proportions. This may be the reason why Francis I had such a strong preference for living there.

The forest of Laye in the Middle Ages was a game reservation without equal. About 1045 Robert le Pieux founded a small monastery there under the patronage of St Germain of Paris. Less than a century later the position of the village, on the edge of the plateau which commands the left bank of the Seine, on the south-east border of wide forests, induced Louis the Fat to build a residence there, since he wished to surround his capital with powerful fortresses. Military considerations were added to the interests and pleasures of a hunter. The building dates to about 1124; it was situated where Charles V's keep now stands, but nothing now remains since it was completely destroyed by the Black Prince in 1346, at the beginning of the Hundred Years War.

The only part of the castle to be spared was the chapel Saint Louis had erected to replace the one built by Philippe-Auguste in 1223. The Sainte-Chapelle, 'finer in both material and art' than its predecessor, may possibly have been built by Pierre de Montreuil, like the other Sainte-Chapelle in Paris, as is usually agreed. This jewel in stone was finished by June 1238. It consists of a long rectangular nave and a polygonal apse. The chapel is flooded with sunlight under its fine pointed arcades, and the vault is supported by groups of delicate columns. The whole is a masterpiece of purity and harmony. It is well known that the keystones of the arches are of great historical interest: they represent St Louis and his family.

This chapel was skilfully repaired at the end of the last century, but many great historical episodes had taken place there. Weddings, for instance: that of Claude of France to Francis of Angoulême, who was to become Francis I; of Marguerite of Angoulême, his sister, the '*Marguerite des marguerites*', to the King of Navarre, Henry IV's grandfather. Christenings too: that of Louis-

Dieudonné, the future Louis XIV, in 1643, and that of the Grand Dauphin in 1668.

After the destruction done by the Black Prince's troops, the castle of St Germain was a mere ruin for several years. Charles V had it rebuilt. Of what was done then all that remains is a strong keep in the north-west corner (1364-1367). Charles V came often to St Germain. Visitors are still shown, on the second floor of the keep, the stone-paved room which was his study: it is now the museum's coin room.

During the civil war the citadel was occupied first by the Burgundians and then by the English; Talbot was its governor in 1434-1435. It was reconquered by the Constable of Richmont. In the fifteenth century, according to Commyns, the Valois were not interested in St Germain and hardly ever came there. Louis XI actually gave it to his doctor, Jacques Coictier, hoping the doctor would then lengthen his life, but the trick did not work and Louis died the next year.

After a sumptuous wedding at St Germain, Francis I decided in 1539 to alter the castle completely. According to Androuet du Cerceau, he thought the place was very pleasant. As early as 1528 he had had a fountain built there, and Pierre Chambiges, who had displayed his skill at Chantilly, was put in charge and worked there until 1544, when he died. One of his near relatives, Guillaume Guillain, succeeded him.

After Francis' death, Henri II gave Philibert Delorme the job of continuing the building; he was replaced in 1559 by Primaticcio. These two architects respected the original designs and ideas of Chambiges and Francis I, 'as the former cared so much for the building of the castle' that Androuet du Cerceau could claim that he was its actual architect.

The main part was finished by 1555. It had cost 136,680 livres during the last eight years of Francis' reign. But the accounts included numerous expenses for decorating the castle afterwards.

The structure had been kept to the foundations of Charles V's castle with the shape of an irregular pentagon. The uniform style of the inner façades is characterized by the use of stone for the main part of the building and of bricks for its decoration. Large arcades on the ground floor and the entresol support a first floor and the balcony, itself surmounted by a lower second floor. The great novelty of St Germain was the roof. It is a huge terrace of stone slabs, and a balustrade decorated with vases. It may be that Chambiges got that idea from a local style of decoration; Charles V's keep was roofed in the same way. To support the great weight of the roof – a stupendous viewpoint from which one looks out upon a wonderful wooded landscape, the windings of the Seine and the whole of Paris – the builders had to use pointed arches in the floor below, and powerful buttresses against the vaults which were strengthened with thick iron bars.

44

Three turrets, opening above the inner courtyard, enclose spiral staircases. They are topped with cupolas.

The originality and harmony of that well-balanced architecture, so typical of the French Renaissance, are less obvious from the outside. For the lower floor the builders kept the military aspect of earlier castles, with a *chemin-de-ronde* around the façade, apart from the chapel and the keep: this was the White Gallery. Above it the Renaissance style is found again, high windows on the first floor and arches on the second. The north front, the longest of all (over 100 yards along the parterre), is pierced in the middle with two superimposed loggias, corresponding to the Grand Staircase by which the terrace is reached.

The originality of St Germain comes from the happy use of alternating stone and brick, and from the terrace and its balustrade, the latter under Italian influence. Philibert Delorme was mostly concerned with St Louis' chapel, the floor of which he raised. This led him to change the interior decoration; he also built an oratory in the park, which has since disappeared.

Francis I and Henri II both liked to visit St Germain. Yet the latter was not completely happy there. East of the old castle lay a wide esplanade ending with a talus leading to the edge of the plateau, from which one looked upon the huge vista of the Seine valley. There, in 1547, the celebrated duel between La Châtaigneraie and Jarnac had taken place, which made the latter famous for the unfair blow he dealt his adversary. Philibert Delorme, who was eager to distinguish himself by building an entirely new work, started on that very spot what he himself called the Theatre and Baths House. He thought of it as a pleasure-house comprising a quadrifoil courtyard surrounded with reception rooms.

Work began in 1557. Two years later the architect fell into disgrace. The building remained unfinished for a long while: at that time it consisted of a central house, with a pavilion at either side, and arcaded galleries. A broad terrace overlooked the Seine. Lawns extended between the two buildings.

It was only under Henri IV that work was resumed. The King had a succession of terraces built between the chateau and Seine, with grottoes hollowed into their foundations. Thomas Francine, an Italian architect whom Henri rewarded by giving him letters of nationalization, installed the famous hydraulic automatons there which delighted the visitors to St Germain for so long: a lady playing the organ, a singing cuckoo, and other admirable devices.

Henceforth, the chateaux of St Germain were fully constituted. Of course, there was still much to do to the interior under Louis XIV. Le Vau and Hardouin-Mansart worked at it, while Le Nôtre planned the flower beds, getting into practice before starting work at Versailles. A few details were changed on the exterior, too, but the main work was done. Then after two centuries of extremely brilliant life, the history of St Germain was one of nothing but long decay.

Yet it was there that Catherine de Medici, Henri II's wife, gave birth to her children. The King came there often. He had even given his mistress, Diane de Poitiers, an apartment on the ground floor below Catherine's. After Henri's death, the Guises ruled over St Germain, where they had established themselves in Charles V's keep. Charles IX ascended the throne in 1560. Many ordinances were signed at St Germain during his reign, and the castle was the scene of several impressive ceremonies. Henri III followed his brothers' example: he lived at St Germain and had a different entertainment devised for each day of the week: a concert on Monday, tennis on Thursday, or a ball on Sunday. Henri IV was the first to prefer living at the Chateau Neuf, keeping the big reception rooms of the Chateau Vieux for state occasions. He installed his mistresses there and all his children, legitimate or illegitimate, who played very noisily in the wing known as the 'Enfants de France'. He liked entertaining friends there, and had Francini's hydraulic automatons play for them. Water flowed in every fountain. The terraces were planted with fruit trees, clipped boxwood arabesques and white mulberry-trees, which Sully and the King were trying to acclimatize.

Louis XIII was born at Fontainebleau, but he was hardly a few weeks old when he came to St Germain for the first time. He was put into the Chateau Vieux, and there he passed his childhood. He hunted every day. Later, he welcomed Richelieu there, whose rooms were situated at the entresol to the Queen's wing. In 1638 he had the very unexpected joy of being presented with an heir by his hitherto barren wife. The event was celebrated with a great ballet, aptly called the 'Felicity Ballet'. Yet, during the last years of his life the King also liked to retire to an unpretentious little manor which he had built within three leagues of St Germain, with a name that now appears in history for the first time: Versailles.

The chateau of St Germain played a leading part during the Fronde. It was there that Anne of Austria retired with her children after the 'Day of the Barricades' in September 1648; she returned to Paris in October. Three months later, at dead of night, she had to flee again, to escape the pressure the Frondeurs were trying to put on her. Mme de Motteville tells us how the royal family had to camp in those big grim halls during an icy night, without beds, furniture, linen or servants, for royalty normally carried all its furniture with them in those days. We knew that this dramatic flight made a deep impression on the young King. Louis XIV never forgave the Parisians for this unpleasant experience. Maybe the destiny of Versailles was settled that very night.

Meanwhile, it is too often forgotten that the whole first part of Louis XIV's reign was passed at St Germain, in the castle which had been more or less happily transformed, first by Francois La Vau, and after 1676 by Jules Hardouin-Mansart. In order to house all the court officers, Mansart built at each corner of the castle, in front of the keep and the chapel, five high pavilions of brick and stone, the ungainly aspect of which ruined the Renaissance façades. Moreover, they were never completed. Some of their floors could be reached only by ladders, since they had no stairs! The Second Empire had them destroyed, as well as the buildings which hid the chapel, obstructed its windows and turned the place into a dismal cellar.

Inside, the ballroom was turned into a theatre, and the various rooms experienced a number of transformations.

However, we owe the happiest creations to Le Nôtre. As early as 1663 he laid out two ornamental beds of clipped boxwood and flowers of varied colours, at right angles to the King's wing. They ended in an ornamental lake, beyond which stretched the road towards Les Loges. Other formal gardens connected the old and the new chateaux, and a bowling green was laid out south of the latter. It was destroyed at the end of the eighteenth century. Finally, Le Nôtre displayed his genius in the creation of the terrace, that beautiful triumphal roadway which overlooks the Seine for over a mile and a half, from the Chateau Neuf to the chateau of Val. Huge supporting walls had to be erected, which consumed 850,000 livres. This masterly work was finished in 1673. As for the forest proper, known as the Great Park, Le Nôtre had 5,585,000 trees planted there in 1664. They knew something about reafforestation in Louis XIV's time!

The King came to St Germain shortly after his wedding in September 1660. He returned the next year, and the court paid longer and more frequent visits to the Château Vieux. In fact, the King's favourite palace was St Germain for some twenty years, while Versailles was being built. There, according to the Grande Demoiselle, who was not always kind, the King had his first intrigue, as a very unfaithful husband, with Mlle de la Motte-Housancourt. There, too, he loved Louise de La Vallière, and afterwards the haughty Diane-Athenais de Mortemart, Marquise de Montespan. She had been given rooms on the ground floor of the Queen's wing, where Diane de Poitiers had lived, for kings are faithful to tradition. It is rather unlikely that Mme de Montespan indulged in witchcraft either there or when staying with her sister, Mme de Thianges: the confessions of a degraded priest and of a poisoner do not carry conviction. In order to soothe the betrayed husband's wrath, Molière wrote in Amphitryon:

> Un partage avec Jupiter
> N'a rien du tout qui déshonore.[1]

In the big ballroom, Louis XIV danced Benserade's *Ballet des Muses* and Molière presented *Mélicerte* or *L'Amour Peintre*. Yet, little by little, the biggest festivities and the most gorgeous ceremonies were transferred to Versailles. The Duc de Saint-Simon was terribly angry at seeing Louis XIV abandoning St Germain. In 1682 the court settled at Versailles for good: 'St Germain, a unique

---

[1] There is nothing dishonourable about sharing a lady with Jupiter.

47

place bringing together a marvellous view, an immense stretch of forest unique for the beauty of its trees, the charm of its gardens, its elevation and its terraces, was abandoned by the King for Versailles, the dullest, and dreariest of all places.'

Yet the Château Vieux was not left unused. It served for the residence of James II Stuart, his queen and their son. This king's catholicism had cost him three kingdoms. The small Stuart court settled at St Germain, vegetating in the hope of a restoration which James' failings soon rendered hopeless. All his attempts failed and he died at St Germain on September 16, 1701, and was buried in the parish church. Together with his mother, Mary of Modena, the young Pretender, known as James III, continued a life without joy or future. With the defeat of his son Charles-Edward at Culloden in 1746, all hope of returning to the throne of England vanished. The last of the Stuarts in the direct line, Henry, Cardinal of York, died in Rome. The last Jacobite had gone from St Germain.

Yet the presence of the Stuarts during the early part of the eighteenth century saved the Château Vieux from ruin. The fate of Château Neuf was deplorable. When the grottoes had been abandoned, Francini's hydraulic automatons quickly fell into disrepair. Jacobite officers had been quartered in the old apartments. Slowly the place was deserted. The buildings were no longer cared for. In 1777 Louis XVI gave the Château Neuf to his brother, the Comte d'Artois, who considered rebuilding the palace, but time passed and the Revolution supervened. All that was done was demolition, and of Château Neuf nothing remains but the Pavilion Henri IV, first given to the Duchess of Courland and Tallyrand and afterwards turned into a hotel, where many well-known people have stayed, among them de Musset and Offenbach; also what is wrongly known as the Pavilion de Sully, a private house, together with the heavy supporting walls and ramps. Lately, a few grottoes have been cleaned out.

The Château Vieux had a very different destiny. The Convention turned it into a political prison. Napoleon established the military school there, the Ecole de Mars. The Restoration turned it into cavalry barracks and a general was given Louis XIV's rooms. We can imagine the state into which the whole building soon fell! Louis-Philippe concentrated on repairing Versailles and did nothing for St Germain, which suffered further humiliation and became a military prison until 1855.

It was Napoleon III who saved the building. He may have felt ashamed at showing Queen Victoria round the former Stuart apartments in their ignominy. In 1862 he decided to have a Celtic and Gallo-Roman Museum established there, which settled the building's fate. Huge works were undertaken. The façades resumed their earlier appearance and all that was done there, until the turn of the century, was quite proper. On the other hand, the interior, in order to turn it into a museum, suffered serious alterations and it is no longer easy to dis-

cover where the apartments were that had undergone such frequent changes since the sixteenth century.

The museum is now in process of complete reorganization and its treasures are being reclassified. No historical event took place in the chateau. The conference which put an end to hostilities between the Allies and the former Austrian monarchy took place at St Germain, and in the Pavilion Henri IV, in the room where Louis XIV was baptised, the Treaty of St Germain was signed on September 10, 1919.

The terrace has kept its splendour, and the flower beds are still enchanting. The forest still surrounds a chateau where part of French history took place and which remains one of the national treasures.

> *De votre Dianet (de votre nom j'appelle*
> *Votre maison d'Anet) la belle architecture*
> *Les arbres animés, la vivante peinture,*
> *Qui le font estimer des maisons la plus belle,*
> *Les beaux lambris dorés, la luisante chapelle,*
> *Les superbes donjons, la riche couverture,*
> *Le jardin tapissé d'éternelle verdure,*
> *Et la vive fontaine à la source immortelle,*
> *Ces ouvrages, Madame, à les bien contempler,*
> *Rapportant de l'antique le plus parfait exemple*
> *Montrent un artifice et dépense admirable. . . .*[1]

This sonnet by Joachim du Bellay, inspired by the wonderful castle of Anet, built for Diane de Poitiers, Henri II's mistress, is a clever list of all the wonders that Philibert Delorme, its architect, managed to accumulate there between 1547 and 1552, to his own greater glory, to the pleasure of the mistress of the house, and for the gaping admiration of all their contemporaries. After four centuries Bellay's verses, among much other praise, are enthusiastic evidence of this admiration.

This masterpiece by the greatest of Renaissance architects was built where a former castle had stood since the early Middle Ages. History has handed down to us the name of the early lords of Anet: they were Robert, Simon or Philippe Urson. In the thirteenth century the castle belonged to the Trénites, and then, in the next century, to Philip V 'the Long'. Thereafter it scarcely left royal possession. That is how it was inherited by Louis d'Evreux. His grandson was the King of Navarre, Charles the Bad, who was so very unreliable that Charles V

[1] The beautiful architecture of your Dianet (I have named your house at Anet after yourself), its life-like marbles, the speaking likeness of the paintings, which make it the most beautiful of houses; the gilded panelling, the shining chapel, the superb keep, the rich roofing, the garden filled with evergreen leaves, and the gay fountain with its immortal spring – all these works, Madame, to those who know how to look at them, are the most perfect imitation of antiquity, and display admirable art and expenditure.

did not hesitate to confiscate the castle. Its defences were dismantled in 1378. In 1445, Charles VII gave what was left as a fief to Pierre de Brézé, who had liberated Normandy from the English. The new owner came from a good family, half-Angevine and half-Norman; he had the castle rebuilt, and also the castle of Brissac in Anjou. He was one of Louis XI's good comrades and died for him in the battle of Montlhéry in 1465.

His son Jacques had married Charlotte, the illegitimate daughter of Agnes Sorel and Charles VII. She was far too free with the young noblemen. Her husband heard of it, surprised her and murdered her, but the King agreed to commute his death sentence and substituted a fine so heavy that Jacques de Brézé could not pay it. He sold Brissac to the Cossé family and returned Anet to the King; but the King gave it back to Louis, the murderer's son. Louis de Brézé took for his second wife Diane, the daughter of Jean de Poitiers and Jeanne de Bastarnay, who was born in 1499. When Louis died, Diane became the adored mistress of Henri II. It was for her that the King had Anet completely rebuilt, and was so interested in the work that 'he was angry when I was not there often enough', wrote Philibert Delorme.

In fact, in five years the great architect built a new castle where Pierre de Brézé's had been constructed in the second half of the fifteenth century. Nothing is left of the earlier castle but a fortified gateway, which shows no evidence of Gothic style at all. It is called Charles the Bad's gate. It is a massive rectangular building of no beauty, having loopholes decorated with gargoyles that look like the mouths of cannon. Probably it was the original castle gateway, and that Diane wanted to preserve both it and its former name, while she made alterations.

The entrance to the new palace is of quite different character. It faces south, and consists of a huge gate, topped by an attic with a terrace at either side. The main gate stands between two smaller ones, framed by doric columns. It has a tympanum with a cast of the well-known reclining Diana, the bronze bas-relief by Benvenuto Cellini, the original of which is now in the Louvre. This high-relief had been ordered by Francis I for Fontainebleau, and Il Rosso made a replica of it for the main gallery of that palace. There were two bronze victories in the corners, but they have disappeared. The attic is surmounted by the figure of a stag, raising its trembling antlers against the sky and surrounded by leaping dogs.

Such is the celebrated Anet gateway, possibly too heavily decorated, but of fine ornamental poise. It was built in 1552: the date appears in one of the niches. The terraces on either side are proof of the architect's skill, as he succeeded in avoiding any appearance of monotony by clever changes in outline. There were pavilions at either end.

The layout of the chateau was very simple. The main building stood at the back of the big courtyard which was flanked by two wings at right angles. On either side, two other courtyards were surrounded by less important buildings.

Little remains of this harmonious whole. The usual pack of vandals was busy there during the First Empire. The triumphal arch of the main building has been re-erected in the courtyard of the Ecole des Beaux-Arts in Paris. As a result of many alterations and additions, it gives a somewhat unsatisfactory idea of the original design. The chapel which formerly was joined to the east wing has vanished. Only the western part of the main building has been preserved.

The chapel is possibly the jewel of Anet. It has the plan of a Greek cross, surmounted by a cupola. Italian influence is obvious. It was decorated by Francisco Scibec, the great cabinet-maker of Anet, and it is graceful and refined. The sculptures are usually ascribed to Jean Goujon. They represent angels bearing the instruments of the Passion or statues of the famous, but the attribution is doubtful. Delorme was the real master at Anet and supervised everything, not hesitating, even on his own admission, to indulge in unashamed splendour, and a quite undeniable display of luxury.

The royal apartments, at the far end of the courtyard, were the first to be built, before 1549, since Scibec was at work on the panelling of the rooms as early as March. The plans which have survived reveal a façade in the French style, to which Philibert Delorme affixed a columned peristyle. He also designed the bay windows, dormer windows of Italian style, and the great portico which is still standing. Later, to enlarge the royal apartments, the architect devised, in the inner angle of the façade overlooking the gardens, a protruding turret, supported by a corbelling vault of extremely intricate design. As he was in doubt as to the reliability of the foundations, he had them strengthened and an underground gallery built the remains of which have been discovered.

As for the western wing, the only one to survive, it was completed on the south by two small watch-towers. At the end of the seventeenth century, the Duc de Vendome altered the façade, pulling down the mullions of the bay-windows and affixing pilasters to the centre. Other alterations were carried out in the nineteenth century and it is now very difficult to reconstruct the internal arrangement of the apartments as they were known to Diane. The grand staircase was built by Claude Desgots and also dates from the time of Louis de Vendôme. Moreover the rooms have changed their functions, but some of Scibec's gilded panelling, and a few precious bits of stained glass, have been preserved. Four magnificent tapestries, woven for Diane's apartments in Fontainebleau and depicting the story of Latona's daughter and the death of Meleager, have been brought back.

It was in the courtyard on the right that the Hunting Diana displayed her splendid nudity above the fountain which bears her name. The statue is now in the Louvre. That it is a daring portrait of the King's mistress is not impossible. The Renaissance knew nothing of prudery.

From glory till death there was but a short interval. Diane herself ordered the funerary chapel in which she intended to be buried. It was built outside the castle proper, has a more classical character with its windowless attic, its triangular front and the sarcophagus which crowns the whole. Just two noble statues, of Faith and Charity, on either side of the entry relieve the austerity of this façade. Diane did not live to see its completion. The tomb was desecrated during the Revolution, but has been well restored recently.

To surround a palace which he rightly regarded as his masterpiece, Philibert Delorme laid out lovely gardens surrounded by galleries. These gardens consisted of very simple, rectangular flower beds. But after Diane's death, her grandson, the Duc d'Aumale, summoned Etienne Pérat, who, together with Claude Mollet, planned areas of flowers surrounded by box, organized nurseries to replace what was destroyed by age or bad weather, and generally built – according to Mollet himself – the very first French parterres, which were soon to become general.

Further changes were carried out in the days of the Duc de Vendóme. Le Nôtre, who delighted in creating large sheets of water, had the Eure partly diverted to fill four canals spreading out at right-angles before reuniting to form the Grand Canal. They surrounded the Ile d'Amour, later planned by the Duchesse du Maine, before forming a glittering waterfall, the sight of which from the terrace is truly enchanting. Next the canal encompasses Diane's garden before rejoining the Eure in two streams. Le Nôtre's parterres and shrubberies have disappeared, but the pools and fountains are still there to mirror the beauty of the Grand Siècle.

Anet belonged to Diane's grandson, the Duc d'Aumale. The chateau was sold in 1615 to Marie de Luxembourg, the Duc de Mercoeur's daughter, who had married César de Vendôme, the illegitimate son of Henri IV and Gabrielle d'Estrées, and it remained in that family for a century. In 1718 it was inherited by the Princesse de Condé, the mother-in-law of the last duke. In 1775, again by inheritance, Anet came to the Duc de Penthièvre, the illegitimate grandson of Louis XIV and Mme de Montespan. It seems that the destiny of a chateau that was built by a royal mistress was always to belong to the illegitimate descendants of the kings. Louis-Philippe owned it for some time in the nineteenth century. But, as we have seen, Diane's chateau had in the meantime been pillaged and torn to pieces.

According to Gébelin, Anet had been Delorme's personal creation; he had wanted to build neither a castle in the French style nor an Italian palace. Thus Anet was one of the most original creations of the Renaissance.

CHAPTER III

ROYAL CHATEAUX OF THE SEVENTEENTH CENTURY

IT IS an interesting fact that two royal chateaux of the seventeenth century owe their creation to the Gondi family. In 1623, Jean-Francois de Gondi, the first Archbishop of Paris, sold to Louis XIII the estate and feudal rights of Versailles which had belonged to his family for half a century. In 1654 the Archbishop's heirs sold to a financier the estate and rights of St Cloud, which were resold four years later by the new owner to Monsieur, the King's brother. But while Louis XIII had already built at Versailles the manor which Saint-Simon contemptuously called a 'card castle', but which was a prelude to the immense construction that was gradually to turn the original building into a magnificent palace, St Cloud was still known for several years as the Gondi's house.

The description was justified: in 1577 Jérôme de Gondi, the Archbishop's grandfather, a good financier and a cunning diplomat in the service of Catherine de Medici, had bought from Jean Rouille, a burgher of Paris, a rather decrepit country house in St Cloud known as the Hotel d'Aulnay. He had it pulled down at once and erected a new residence erected a little further away, on the slope of the hill above the Seine. The new house, in the classical style, consisted of a central building with two short wings, one on each side. On the left, a corner tower connected the main building and the wing. The façades were decorated with statues, columns and bas-reliefs. Monumental chimneys, gathered into clusters to look like Greek vases, ornamented the roofs. On the left, a balcony opened upon the whole panorama of the Seine, but the outstanding source of delight, and what made Jérôme de Gondi's house renowned, were the terraced gardens and the scenic waterworks he had organized.

Alas! This little palace was soon the scene of a tragedy. Henri III, while besieging Paris, then held by the League, which refused to admit him, was living at Gondi's house. On August 1, 1589, a monk asked to see him, claiming that he bore an important message. We know what happened next: how Brother Jacques Clement, thrusting his knife into the royal stomach, gave the throne of France to Henri of Navarre, who became Henri IV.

The stains of blood were quickly effaced. Jérôme de Gondi's sons had to sell the chateau in 1687. Jean-François bought it back eight years later. Was it Jean-François or one of his predecessors who altered the waterworks? We only know that the Gondis had them built by the best Italian engineer, Thomas Francini, who was soon to be given the proud title of 'General Supervisor of His Majesty's Grottoes and Waterworks'. It is obvious that he had tried his hand out at St Cloud. He had built fountains there, the water from the fountains was used to make an organ play, prefiguring the organ-playing lady of St Germain.

The Archbishop was immensely proud of his gardens. He often invited foreigners to visit them, and collected an entrance fee (fifteen sols for the waterworks; thirty for the castle and gardens). A rhyming lawyer described the wonders to be seen at St Cloud at some length:

> Ma Muse de St Cloud veut faire son Parnasse,
> C'est sur ce tertre ici je veux qu'elle trace
> Non les sacrés palais des princes et des rois,
> Mais la sombre épaissur de ces superbes bois,
> Ces larges promenoirs, ces noires enfonçures,
> Ces cabinete secrets, ces retraites obscures,
> Où règnent à l'envie mille divinités,
> Ces grottes où les sens se trouvent enchantés,
> Ces parterres divers, ces riches broderies,
> Ces tranquilles canaux et ces vertes prairies
> Dont les tapis troublants et parfumés de fleurs,
> Etalent a nos yeux tant de vives couleurs. . . .[1]

Louis XIII came several times to St Cloud. Yet, when the Archbishop died his heirs – a brother who was General of the Galleys, and his nephew – preferred to sell the castle to a rich financier, Barthelemy d'Hervart, who saw a chance of good profit. He merely maintained the waterworks, bought some more land and enjoyed the view for four years. Then, at Mazarin's suggestion, he sold the estate to Monsieur, Louis XIV's brother, on October 26, 1658, for 250,000 livres. He had bought it for 72,000; a highly profitable venture.

Gondi's House, as it was still called, became the scene of royal receptions, banquets and visits by the young King to Monsieur and his friends. Monsieur brought his young wife, Henrietta Stuart, after their wedding on March 31, 1661. Henrietta, whose marriage was a failure, lived mostly at St Cloud; she often entertained the King and flirted with him. The Queen Mother intervened. Then Henrietta took the Comte de Guiche as a lover.

[1] My Muse of St Cloud would make her Parnassus. On this hillock I wish that she would trace not the sacred palaces of princes and kings, but the sombre depths of those splendid woods, those large dark glades, those dark hollows and secret towers, these hidden retreats, where a thousand deities reign in fancy, those grottoes where the senses are enchanted, those varied flower-beds with their rich embroideries, those tranquil canals and green meadows, thick with perfumed flowers, stretching so many brilliant colours before our eyes. . . .

St Cloud, the 'abode of rest and joy', became the goal of court excursions. So far it had changed little. Monsieur wanted to build a larger palace and more to his own taste, but he was short of money. So he had to content himself with extending his estate by buying the neighbouring orchards and fields and having flowers and clusters of trees planted. At the same time, he entrusted Antoine Le Pautre with the task of altering the Gondis' big waterfall and giving it a grander setting. Work began in 1163 and was completed four years later. Bernini, who saw St Cloud in 1665, confined his admiration to the waterworks: '*E bella!*' *E bella!*' he remarked.

It was not without grandeur: the cascade was supported by a big wall topped by a balustrade, at the centre of which were two recumbant statues, representing the Loire and the Seine. Further statues alternated with the fountains that surrounded the main central water pillar. Seven ramps came down by stages to the basins where the water was collected; they were decorated with flower vases and with lawns on either side. Vases and fountains alternated skilfully, leading to the basins from which water rose again in glittering jets. This water, so skilfully tamed by Le Pautre, gave life to the stone framework. Louis XIV inaugurated the Grand Cascade in May 1667.

In the chateau Henrietta tried to forget the neglect of a husband who merely got her with child every year; she complained of it to her friend, Mme de La Fayette, to whom she dictated her memoirs. Again she had fugitive meetings with Guiche. She gave herself up to the mediocre pleasures of the table. The King cared for her no longer. At Versailles the haughty Marquise de Montespan was triumphant. When he was not with the army, Monsieur was happy only in the company of the Chevalier de Lorraine. Embittered by this odious life, Henrietta agreed to go as ambassadress to Charles II in an attempt to detach England from her alliance with the Dutch. She was successful and came back to St Cloud in June 1670. On the evening of the 29th she was suddenly siezed by a terrible pain in her side and died on the 30th in great pain. Boussuet was near her at the end. It did not appear that she had been poisoned: severe appendicitis followed by peritonitis may have killed her.

She was soon forgotten. As early as November 1671, Monsieur married his second wife, Elisabeth-Charlotte of Bavaria, a Palatine Princess. St Cloud had to be cleansed of the scandals, intrigues and unpleasant recollections which vitiated its atmosphere. After having signed more than 120 contracts for enlarging the park, Monsieur at last made up his mind: in 1676 Jean Hardouin-Mansart was ordered to build the new chateau at the top of the hill. The main building was done by Girard, who assisted him.

Nothing is left of the new chateau but some engravings and prints. Its general layout is known; the wings were built first and were almost more important (especially the left wing) than the main building, in which were Monsieur's apartments and the chapel. The decorations were done by Mignard, Nocret and

Rousseau. The first-floor of the right wing was almost completely occupied by the Apollo gallery, painted by Mignard. The whole of mythology had been concentrated on its ceilings, canopy and walls. The gallery led to the Diana salon at right angles, also decorated by Mignard. On the other side, next to the royal apartment, was the Mars salon. Madame's apartments were on the first floor of the left wing. The salon at the far end was the work of Nocret. It is useless to describe rooms of which nothing remains but the memory, but one might recall that in the space between the windows of the Apollo gallery Mignard had painted the finest royal chateaux and their gardens–St Germain, Versailles, Fontainebleau, Vincennes, Chambord and Villers-Cotterêts. It is easy to understand why, after having looked at all those masterpieces, Louis XIV said to the Palatine Princess: 'I do hope, Madam, that the paintings in my gallery at Versailles will be as beautiful as yours. . . .'

In October 1678 the old Gondi house was pulled down, although the other palace was not yet complete. While Mignard and Nocret organized the decoration of the apartments at leisure, while the walls were furnished with tapestries and the rooms with pieces of furniture, Le Nôtre was laying out new gardens, altering them according to Monsieur's fancy and his new acquisitions. The proximity of the Seine and the slope of its land, even though the park lay mostly on the plateau, did not make his task easier. Immediately below the chateau, Apollo's gardens put a triangle of flowers and fountains on the right side of the buildings. A statue of Flora was surrounded by dancing nymphs. Parallel to this was a mysterious maze which Monsieur's guests used to visit with chosen friends. On the left, a fountain-lined alley, the Allée des Goulettes, led to the Rocailles spring. Below, the Salle des Maroniers spread its leafy dome. Behind stood the Orangery, and then the forest, with its beautiful foliage, provided a frame to an octagonal esplanade, surrounded with fountains, in the middle of which the Gerbe scattered its sparkling drops. Finally, beyond the Tapis Vert, the Grande Gerbe spouted as high as the tallest trees.

The lower gardens displayed equally surprising hydraulic effects, and visitors came from afar to admire the Great Fountain which rose to the height of a hundred feet, and the Migardise, the Gros Bouillon, and above all, on the left, the carp pond and the Grande Cascade. The latter was rebuilt in 1669 by Mansart, who doubled its size. A second waterfall beyond the Allée du Tillet was lined with statues, and ran down to the lower gardens. It collected the water of the first through underground pipes. Increased in that way, the Grande Cascade became a wonder and a source of attraction to crowds of Parisians and foreigners, whom Monsieur allowed to walk freely in the gardens.

This, however, was Monsieur's last achievement at St Cloud. Overcome with melancholy, he immersed himself in bigotry. Looking at the works of art he had accumulated, he would say to the Chevalier de Lorraine: "I look upon these fine rooms and those beautiful gardens, and think how I shall have to leave them!" Indeed, on June 8, 1701, driving back from Marly after yet another quarrel with Louis XIV, who had blamed him for the profligacy of his son the Duke of Chartres, Philip of Orléans suffered a stroke and died the next day at noon.

Inheriting the title, his son, the new Duke of Orleans, left the chateau to his mother, the Palatine Princess, and scarcely returned except to entertain some friends to dinner or to a concert. Peter the Great of Russia visited him there in 1717, but it has been said that the princess pleased him more than the buildings. When the Regent died, the chateau passed to his brother Louis, who slightly altered the gardens and pulled down the water-walk of les Goulettes; he also repaired the Grande Cascade, which was on the verge of collapse. In 1734, the sculptor Lambert Adam decorated it with new statues.

For the greater part of the eighteenth century St Cloud remained the property of the Orleans. Louis-Philippe-Joseph merely added a few paintings by Coypel. Following the advice of his mistress, Mme de Montessan, he sold the estate to Marie-Antoinette in 1785 for six million livres. He kept the furniture, paintings and works of art.

The Queen at once commissioned her usual architect, Mique, to transform the interior completely; in her view it was no longer in keeping with contemporary taste. Except for the Mars room, the Diana room and the Apollo Gallery, all the apartments were re-decorated and completely refashioned: walls were covered with lacquer, panelling and light silk. The gardens were changed in the same way, so that the Queen might pretend she was a milkmaid in the Pavillon de la Laiterie, and dream of rural bliss in the Pavillon de la Félicité.

The Revolution put an end to all these rustic pleasures. Sometimes the King and the Queen repaired to St Cloud to rediscover a little of the Versailles atmosphere, but when the monarchy had fallen, the park was opened to the public and the furniture auctioned.

A lean and ambitious general led France back to peace through dictatorship. St Cloud was the stage on which the Eighteenth Brumaire was enacted. The members of the Conseil des Anciens and Conseil des Cinq-Cents had taken refuge in the hastily furnished Orangery to escape the pressure of armed troops. Bonaparte appeared and scattered the useless talkers. The Consulate was born.

Was it because of its association with his triumph that Bonaparte often returned to the palace? He had the interior restored, the waterworks rebuilt and Demosthenes' lantern erected (a copy of the one on the Acropolis) at the end of the Grande Allée. The apartments were filled with Empire furniture, gorgeous and heavy. David's paintings were hung everywhere. Talma acted on a stage built where Monsieur's former theatre had stood.

A few historical events took place there: after Napoleon's marriage to Marie-Louise, the Archduchess entered the drawing-rooms which had been inhabited by her aunt Marie-Antoinette. Louis-Napoleon, Queen Hortense's son, who became Napoleon III, was baptised at St Cloud; so was the King of Rome. Napoleon went there for the last time in 1813.

The chateau brought no luck to its inhabitants. Louis XVIII and Charles X did not stay there long. The latter was there when he signed the celebrated decrees which brought about the Revolution of 1830 and the fall of the legitimate monarchy. It was from St Cloud that Charles X left to go into exile.

Louis-Philippe was an Orleans; the chateau had belonged to his family and it was his great-grandfather who had built it. Yet he found a place which had altered very much and in which various styles did not blend well. He did not try to create something new. He restored and cleaned soiled paintings, repaired the Grande Cascade once more, put a riding school in the Orangery and allowed a railway to cross the park.

Under Napoleon III St Cloud became the favourite summer residence of the sovereigns. At big receptions the chateau came to life again. There the Emperor entertained the defeated Abd-el-Kader, as well as Queen Victoria and the King of Sweden. There was one tragic encounter, when the half-demented Empress Charlotte begged the Emperor in vain to help her husband Maximilian, who had been launched upon the fatal Mexican venture.

On July 28, 1870, Napoleon and the Prince Impérial left St Cloud to take command of the army. They never returned. On September 19th a shower of shells from Mont Valerien fell upon the chateau, which was entirely destroyed by fire a month later. For twenty years its gutted ruins stood against the sky. They were razed at last in 1891.

The park remains. It spreads its beautiful trees over the plateau between Sèvres, Ville-d'Avray, Garches and St Cloud. Century-old trees of many kinds still enable visitors to stray along the winding paths and conjure up the shadows of the past. The Francini fountains, the Le Pautre and Mansart waterfalls have retained their beauty. Statues have disappeared, but the Grand Jet still throws its waters high. Those noble gardens, the only witnesses of a vanished past, remind the passer-by of the vanity of human enterprise.

In 1632 Louis XIII bought the Versailles estate from Jean-Francois de Gondi. The King's servants hammered in poles stamped with the fleur-de-lis to fix the boundaries of his land. In a way this gesture was the birth certificate of the Palace of Versailles.

Versailles is by far the most illustrious of all royal palaces. It symbolizes the monarchy in all its pomp and grandeur. The personal creation of the last four Bourbon kings, it does not have its roots in the deepest historical past, like Fontainebleau or St Germain-en-Laye. Gondi's chateau at Versailles was a mere ruin without a past. Louis XIII did not even erect his manor where it had stood. On the low hill where the manor was to stand, there was then nothing but a windmill.

The circumstances in which it was built have often been recorded. It would have been hard for another king to put up with 'this thankless place, without a view, without water, without soil', as Saint-Simon put it. If Saint-Simon were to return today, he would be astonished by the crowds which, every day, even in the dead of winter, flock to visit the palace and admire the park. Louis XIII loved hunting and solitude and this big village on the road to Normandy was to his liking. As early as 1624 he had a house built there; for him it was something of a hermitage. There were about twenty rooms in the two-storied main building flanked by two small wings at right angles towards the east. When he had bought the estate, Louis XIII asked his architect Philibert le Roy to enlarge the older house. Philibert completely rebuilt the front over the courtyard in brick with lines of white stone, and he erected four little pavilions at the four outer angles. Towards the east, Boyceau was already laying out the first parterres.

The courtiers regarded Versailles merely as a hunting lodge. When Louis XIII died, and for about ten years thereafter, no one knew for certain what would happen to the little manor. Louis XIV made only fleeting appearances, for he was more often at St Germain. Yet he thought that he must leave posterity some relic of his reign. He admired Mazarin's palace and the splendour of Vaux. So in 1661, shortly after Fouquet's arrest (it is edifying to put the two dates side by side), he made up his mind. Le Nôtre was appointed master-builder. The terrain had, in fact, to be prepared for planning the park. A large ornamental flower bed stretched in front of the façade. The round swan pond was a first version of the Apollo basin. Le Nôtre made his geometry fit the lie of the land. The park, at the back of which stood the palace, was covered with statues and vases enlivened by fountains devised by Francini. The castle proper was redecorated by Errard and Coypel. Outhouses arose. In 1664, *Les Plaisirs de l'Île enchantée* provided the courtiers with the most sumptuous entertainment in honour of a young, handsome king, who was then in love. In 1668, other and even more staggering entertainments took place when the victorious treaty of Aix-la-Chapelle was signed.

Then the King launched himself into major works. In spite of Colbert's advice, according to whom nothing great could be built at Versailles, the King entrusted La Vau with the task. The architect kept the early chateau; but he provided the centre with a balcony and extended a wing at either side. The slated roofs were replaced by terraced roofs decorated with balustrades, trophies and vases. This Italian decoration enchanted the King and suited Le Nôtre's vistas perfectly.

On the side of the Marble Court, while retaining the original architecture, Le Vau built long parallel pavilions which enclosed wide courtyards. Quarters had to be found for the royal family and the courtiers. After La Vau's death in 1670, his pupil Dorbay completed the task. Painters and sculptors decorated the interior under the supervision of Le Brun, the life and soul of that vast workshop. At the same time, the hamlet of Versailles was becoming a town. Wide avenues, branching off starlike from the chateau, were lined with fine private houses. The new town, round the future parish of Notre-Dame, was growing up north of the palace.

After having reigned over the King's heart, Louise de la Vallière gave place to Mme de Montespan. Athenäis de Rochechouart-Mortemart, full of wit and pride, was the real Queen of Versailles. In spite of the war which the Coalition; led by the Dutch, was waging against the Most Christian King, new festivals were held to proclaim the King's fame and the grandeur of his palace to the far corners of the earth.

Nevertheless, Louis XIV was not satisfied. He was now thinking of settling the seat of government itself at Versailles. It was therefore indispensable to enlarge the palace, and in 1678 Mansart was given this difficult task.

This great architect was full of imagination and ingenuity, but also of precision and conscience. For thirty years he worked with the King and gave the palace its final aspect. Where Le Vau had built his long terrace, between two pavilions, he erected the Hall of Mirrors between 1678 and 1687. Le Brun painted the ceilings, commemorating the victories in the war against Holland. Between 1679 and 1680 he altered the façade of the Marble Court and connected the two separate pavilions above the courtyard, creating what are known as the Ministers' Wings. Finally, he immensely extended the central body of the palace, erecting the Aile du Midi (the South Wing, 1678-1681) and the Aile du Nord (the North Wing, 1687-1689) to house the royal family and the princes. The first was destined for the princes of the blood and the legitimised bastards – they were many, for Mme de Montespan had given Louis XIV seven children – and for the noblemen of the Court.

That was not all. The chateau had become a huge city which had to be fed. Consequently, where the old village had stood Mansart erected between 1681 and 1687 the Grand Commun, where all the victualling services were housed: kitchens, bread store, butler's stores, etc. The cavalry had also to be accommodated, as the early stables had become inadequate. At the point whence the three avenues radiate from the esplanade, the Great Stables and the Small Stables were soon to reveal their perfect semi-circle. The Great Stables, thanks to their classical harmony, their perfect balance, the skill with which they were planned, may well be Mansart's masterpiece.[1]

There was more to come. In 1682 Louis XIV had established all the government offices at Versailles, where he had settled his own residence, which did not prevent him from visiting other royal chateaux. But the work went on among the rubble, while hundreds of workmen were still completing Mansart and Le Nôtre's grandiose designs. Towards the south, in front of the wing that had been

[1] They are now the departmental archives.

built, the sudden collapse of the terrain was an unpleasant sight; Mansart solved the problem ingeniously. He built a terrace under which between 1681 and 1686 he laid out the new Orangery, formed by a wide gallery with high, arched windows. The King of Siam remarked: 'Louis XIV must be very rich indeed to erect such a wonderful building to house orange trees!' On either side, two staircases (the Hundred Steps or the Grand Degrés), flank the building and give access to the Pièce d'Eau des Suisses, the still waters of which extend to the wooded hills surrounding the park.

All this was transformed under Le Nôtre's direction. The master gardener never relaxed. The Grand Canal with its two branches was given the aspect we now know, and a whole flotilla with sailors in many-coloured costumes enabled the King to offer the ladies concerts or refreshments on the water. Basins were built and decorated with mythological statues, the work of famous sculptors and founders – Coysevox, Le Hongre, Marsy or Tuby. Between 1685 and 1688 the famous colonnade and its big fountains were erected. It is made of thirty-two columns of white, pink and blue marble, surrounding basins from which fountains rise.

The waters and stones of Versailles have been celebrated so often that one hesitates to evoke them once again. Yet are they not the most original aspects of the park, these many mirroring sheets of water at various levels, reflecting the changing colours of the sky, the stones of the palace or the statues that surround them? The expanse of water in front of the façade, the Latone basin, the Apollo basin, and especially near the northern flower beds, the water avenue of twenty-two small basins of white marble leading to the Dragon basin, and to the majestic Neptune basin above all? It was begun by Le Nôtre and Mansart in the reign of Louis XIV and not completed until 1740. It has been said that the whole park is a tribute to the god of waters, the waters which had been so hard to bring there.

Those countless basins on either side of the Tapis Vert never were – either then or now – pools of dead water – the phrase coined by Mlle de Scudery. They were enlivened by the 1,400 jets of water that threw their waters skyward. Only 670 of them remain today.

As a unique setting to the waters, the stones and bronzes of Versailles deserve to be mentioned. Again, we have to list the names of Le Brun, Mansart, Mignard, Coysevox, Le Hongre and the founder Tuby. The latter was responsible for the reclining statues of the water gods, the Saône and the Rhône, while Le Hongre sculpted the Seine and the Marne; Coysevox created the Garonne and the Dordogne. Beautiful marble and bronze vases complete the decoration.

You discover the Versailles statues one by one, as you stroll along the glades and avenues. Le Hongre or Coysevox's nymphs, sculpted in pink-veined marble, have an undescribable charm. The gods and goddesses of the Diana fountain seem to form a triumphant escort to the King and his Court. One should also mention the well-known group in the Latone basin by Balthasar Marsy, or Tuby's Chariot of Apollo and the Flora group.

It is easy to understand why Louis XIV was proud of his work and why he wrote a booklet about the way the gardens should be seen. He really did take visitors round himself.

Yet the most powerful of kings sometimes needed to relax. He felt a longing to set aside for a time the pompous majesty in which he lived, the minutely regulated ceremonial and the rigorous etiquette. His rest house, a pink marble palace where human dimensions were substituted for the majestic, was the Grand Trianon.

Louis XIV had built it – so he said himself – for his own pleasure. Erected by Hardouin-Mansart, it replaced the Trianon de Porcelaine, a delightful little pavilion adorned with floral decorations. It was more imposing but, with a peristyle of pink and green marble and a simple, unadorned façade, it is the embodiment of discreet luxury. Its terraced roof is edged with a balustrade formerly decorated with vases and sculptures.

The right wing faces the King's gardens, less pompous than those of the main palace. Here were the King's and Mme de Maintenon's apartments. In the slightly more recent left wing were the Mirror room, the chapel and the Princes' room.

The Grand Trianon dates from 1687 and it is possible that Hardouin-Mansart had had assistance in completing it. The last building added to the main palace was the chapel, in the centre of the north wing, where it raises its wide and majestically-proportioned nave, with aisles and no transept, ending in a semicircular apse. Mansart did not live to see it finished; it was completed by Robert de Cotte, his brother-in-law, and dedicated in June 1710 by the Archbishop of Paris. The difficulties of the times made it impossible to decorate the chapel as richly as had been planned. Yet this 'House of God in the King's Palace', according to a well-known description, was still very grand, and when the court crowded there to see the King as much as to pray, the scene was gorgeous.

Times were hard and Versailles very dull. Youth had departed. The Marquise de Montespan, whose name had been too notorious at the time of the 'Poison Affair', had retired into piety. Another woman had stepped into her shoes: the Marquise de Maintenon who was soon to rule over the King's heart; she married him later.

We shall probably never know the actual date when the wedding took place and it does not matter very much. What is certain is that the woman who replaced Maria-Theresa wielded a major influence at court. She knew how to keep her rank with tact, but she gave the King a taste for more intimate entertainments. This born schoolmistress grew passionately fond of her creation, the school of St Cyr. This 'lady with an endless cold' – the nickname Mme de Sévigné gave her – was freezing to death in the ice-cold galleries. During the terrible War of the Spanish Succession bread made from oats was eaten at Versailles, and the King sent his silver plate to the mint. Mme de Maintenon and Fénelon were for peace in defeat, but Louis XIV would not agree. The situation righted itself eventually. The reign ended, if not in joy, at least in serenity.

The alterations to the chateau of Versailles went on, which is why it is so difficult today to discover how it was furnished. During the following century tastes changed immensely. Apart from the building of the Opera under the influence of the Marquise de Pompadour, who was for twenty years the 'minister of arts and pleasures', we pass from the Great King's solemn sumptuousness to the fluid grace of rococo, from fixed lines to curved ones. Furniture was light and full of elegance, and François Lemoyne and Verbeck d'Anvers altered their earlier aspect. The former, who has been rightly called a 'disturber of Olympus' carved out in the ceiling of the Hercules Room a lively representation of gods and goddesses amidst delicate clouds. The Music Room, made for Mme Adélaide, the King's daughter, was decorated with rustic emblems. Cabinet-makers like Cressent and Oeben made chiffoniers, secretaires and consoles in keeping with smaller, more intimate, more comfortable rooms. Oudry, Boucher, Nattier or Latour, with their exquisite paintings, made women triumphant at Versailles.

The Marquise de Pompadour's rooms were on the second floor, in an apartment overlooking the north garden, and the King had access to it by a small secret staircase. The courtiers who were not invited to the Marquise's parties usually spoke of her rooms as 'garrets' or 'rat holes'. It was mere peevishness that made them speak thus, for these rooms were exquisitely furnished and decorated, as we can still see, for they have been restored with complete fidelity. Louis XV himself had given up his great-grandfather's bedroom (in which he caught cold) and had a room made for himself by Verbeckt, opening upon the Marble Court. Nearby was the Clock Chamber, named after Passement's fantastic clock, which still chimes the hours, either propitious or not. At the end of the wing the corner room faces the big courtyard, from the balcony of which, on an April evening in 1764, Louis XV, with tears running down his cheeks, watched the funeral procession of the Marquise de Pompadour.

A reign was drawing to its end. The Marquise had not seen the completion of the Trianon which Louis XV had built for her. It was another royal mistress, Jeanne du Barry, who was to open it. Gabriel had built it between 1762 and 1768: truly a little palace, with a raised ground-floor and an attic with tiny windows. The pert style was strongly accentuated by the four columns which reached to the cornice.

Jacques-Ange Gabriel, the King's leading architect from 1742 on, had succeeded his father, Jacques Gabriel, who in his turn had replaced Robert de Cotte in 1735. The son became the great Versailles architect of the eighteenth century. Not all his creations were equally happy, and the wing he built in 1771-74, that protruded into the courtyard between the chateau and the chapel, is one of the regrettable additions which wreck the balance sought by Mansart. The four columns on its façade, supporting a heavy pediment, are lacking in grace. This wing and the one which the architect Dufour built in 1820 to face it spoil the majesty of the palace. They break the perspectives. They antagonise many visitors who are struck by their poor design when they first see the Palace of Versailles from the Avenue de Paris. Similarly, one may deplore the loss of the great Ambassadors' Staircase that once gave such a fine approach to the galleries leading to the chapel.

On the other hand, Gabriel gave us the Opera, which was solemnly opened for the wedding of the Dauphin and Marie-Antoinette in 1770. The renovation of this theatre, which may well be the most beautiful in the world, has restored to Versailles one of its noblest masterpieces. Its discreet elegance and the balance of its proportions are a delight to the eye. The main colour is blue, delicately balanced by the pale pink of the columns and the gilded sculptures. On the ceiling Durameau painted *Apollo crowning illustrious men*. The sculpted decoration was the work of Pajou. Henceforth, all the great court ceremonies took place in this refined and sumptuous setting.

Under Louis XV changes were made to the park too. The Neptune basin had never been finished. It was completely altered in 1739 after a competition. Lambert Adam made a central group for it in which Neptune and Amphritite are surrounded by nereids, tritons, horses and marine monsters. They all threw jets of water up into the sky. In the corners another group by Bouchardon represents dragons led by cupids, and the impressive décor is completed by leaden vases.

Other groves were redecorated. The old marsh was turned into a garden for the Dauphin, with statues by the two Coustous: Jupiter was given the features of Louis XV and Juno those of Marie-Leczinsky.

There was an attempt to return to nature, a fashionable pursuit of the period. The highly formal groves which bordered the walk were replaced by fully growing trees. Beyond Trianon the Menagerie was built (1750) with a cowshed, a sheepfold and a dairy which actually brought some rural atmosphere into the park. Nearby, Gabriel built the Pavillon Français, the harmonious grace of which is surrounded by the gardens he also evolved with consummate 'galantry', alternating flower beds and basins. Verdant groves were connected one with the other by little winding alleys which replaced the straight paths of earlier days. Beyond was the botanical garden, carefully tended by Claude Richard and his son Antoine, under Jussieu's supervision.

The chateau was not greatly altered under Louis XVI and Marie-Antoinette. When compelled by etiquette, the new King and Queen kept to the State Apartments, and Marie-Antoinette's children were born in Marie-Leczinska's room. But she preferred to live in the Little Apartments planned for her by her architect Richard Mique, Gouthiere or the Rousseau brothers. This suite of rooms, between the Queen's Apartments, facing the South Courtyard, and the King's,

are fresh and graceful. It was in her little south room that the Queen used to receive her dressmaker Mlle Bertin and her tempting fabrics.

But there were times of relaxation at the Petit Trianon and the Hameau. In a charming way, Louis XVI said to the Queen: 'These beautiful places have always been the abode of the Kings' favourites; therefore they must be yours.' The Petit Trianon was decorated and furnished with exquisite taste under Mique's supervision. The Queen's presence remains, for the furniture that she chose has been carefully restored to the room, and the Empress Eugénie, who was devoted to the Queen's memory, personally cared for it.

But the last Bourbon Queen of France mostly left her mark on the new layout of the gardens. We must leave specialists to discuss the exact origin of the so-called 'English' gardens. One thing is certain, that in the second half of the eighteenth century the gardens of Versailles were profoundly altered and the park we now see and admire little resembles what it was under Louis XIV. The old maze had already been turned into the Grove of Venus, having arbours surrounded by sinuous walks and planted with exotic trees. The old grove of Apollo's Baths had been completely altered in accordance with Hubert Robert's plan. A rock was hollowed out to form a cave to house the groups of statuary. Walks surrounded the rock, and spreading out from it were sheets of water tumbling into a little lake. This over-elaborate affair was completed in 1779.

By that time the Petit Trianon gardens had been created under the supervision of Mique and Richard, after the drawings of the Comte de Caraman, whose fine creations the Queen had admired in Paris. The design was simple and harmonious. The river flowed round a mound on the top of which stood a belvedere decorated by Deschamps with trophies representing the emblems of Love and Gardening, for at this time these two pastoral pleasures were often associated. Mique had a grotto hollowed out, put bridges over the river, and in the middle of an island built the Temple of Love, where a cupola with a perfect curve rests upon twelve corinthian columns. The 'English' garden surrounds the structures Mique erected for the Queen and her friends after 1782: the Queen's house, the Bailly's house, Marlborough's tower, the mill, the dairy, the farm. Thatches covered those slight and charming structures, which perfectly reflected the sweetness of an epoch that was coming to an end.

In her Little Theatre the Queen and her 'Company of Lords' acted the *Le barbier de Séville* or *Le devin du village*. It was into this hamlet that the Queen liked to retire to forget politics and intrigues. The tragi-comedy of the Diamond Necklace may have made her aware of how far public opinion was against her. The consequences of that scandal chastened her. She lived more for her children, and Mme Vigée-Lebrun often painted her with the Dauphin and Madame Royale. Such were the last peaceful hours at Versailles, from which the royal family was to be dragged in the early days of October 1789, when a screaming

E

mob came to demand, under the chateau windows, the 'baker', the 'baker's wife' and the 'little apprentice'.

The Revolution passed over the palace without too much damage to the structure, but all the furniture was doubtless auctioned off. The park, which served as the scene of revolutionary festivities, was left in a pitiful state: the Grand Canal was full of mud, and grass grew everywhere, and a tavern had been put into the Pavillon Français! However, as early as the Consulate, restoration was in hand and continued during the First Empire. Madame Mère, Napoleon's mother, settled into the Grand Trianon and refurnished it. Thanks to Pauline Borghese, the Petit Trianon recovered its charm.

During the Restoration the architects Dufour and Fontaine continued the work. The first erected the heavy wing, symmetrical with Gabriel's. The second restored the Hall of Mirrors, the State Apartments and the Marble Court their former aspect. Fontaine also restored the chapel. Yet Louis XVIII and Charles X only paid fleeting visits to Versailles, for it was full of unhappy memories.

Louis-Philippe settled the fate of the palace by deciding its eventual function. He turned it into a 'conservatorium for the works of art collected in its magnificent galleries'. It was dedicated to 'All the Glories of France' and was formally opened on March 10, 1837. The architects of the July Monarchy are rightly blamed for having thoughtlessly destroyed and transformed the interior to organize the museum. There were irreparable losses: woodwork and bronzes were replaced by plain panels. The Galerie des Batailles, in the south aisle, built by Fontaine and Nepveu, does not stand comparison with the Galerie des Glaces. And yet, several of the small apartments, those of Louis XVI and Marie-Antoinette and the little rooms on the second floor, were preserved, and one must be grateful to Louis-Philippe for having saved the chateau of Versailles and the peerless collection of buildings which surrounds it.

For more than a century the curators have been attempting to restore the chateau tactfully. Crowds flock to the palace which has always served as a setting for great historical events, such as the proclamation of the German Empire in January 1871, and the signature of the Treaty of Versailles in June 1919. No foreign sovereign coming to Paris ever failed to be taken to Versailles, whether Queen Victoria or the Czar of all Russias. Thus the chateau of Versailles remains intimately bound up with history of France, and the Grand Trianon, in order to welcome its guests, has been the object of the most skilful restoration.

'Finally, worn out with splendour and crowds, the King sometimes took refuge in humility and solitude.' This sentence from Saint-Simon is less often quoted than his furious denunciation of Versailles. But it is just as false. For the group of pavilions at Marly had nothing humble about them. And the King never went there alone. He himself gave the lie to that statement. 'I had Marly built for the courtiers,' he proclaimed.

Such a strange choice has caused astonishment. Before the days of Louis XIV, Marly was a fairly important town, on the margin of the forest between Versailles and St Germain. There were two churches, that of the town, at the foot of the hill, which was the older, and that of the chateau itself, at the top of the hill. The chateau was built in a north-south orientation, more or less parallel to the Seine, and about half a league away from it. The estate belonged at the time to François Boussuet.

It had long been in the hands of the Montmorencys. By the middle of the fourteenth century it had passed over to the Lévis and then, at the end of the sixteenth century, to the Gondis, whom we find here again, just as we did at St Cloud and Versailles. It was the Archbishop of Paris and his brother who in 1655 sold the barony of Marly to François Boussuet for 153,000 livres, 23 sols and 14 deniers. Finally, in 1676, Louis XIV bought the barony of Marly-le-Chatel which he united to his Versailles estate. There was scarcely anything there but the bare ground; the Montmorency's old keep was a ruin.

As for the neighbouring estate of Marly-le-Bourg, it belonged in 1689 to Phélippeaux de Pontchartrain. The King's secretary was only too glad to please his master by exchanging it in June 1693 for the estate of Neauphle.

By that time building at Marly had been going on for a long time. It seems that the first clearing of the ground took place in June 1679 or a little earlier. Cartloads of earth had to be brought to level the uneven surface, on which it was difficult to draw the wide lines and long vistas the King loved. Thousands of carts, laden with stones, had to come up from Port-Marly, on the banks of the Seine, over the side of the Coeur-Volant. Workmen came from the Ile-de-France and also from provinces like the Limousin and the Marche. Local peasants had to do forced labour too. At one time even soldiers of the King's regiments were put to work. In the Marly parish registers too many traces can be found of fatal accidents occurring on the vast scaffoldings.

It is fairly easy to decide when work began, but quite impossible to state when it was complete. It is not sufficiently known that Louis XIV became very fond indeed of Marly, almost as much as he was of Versailles. He never ceased changing it. In 1699, 1700 and 1701, he even spent more on Marly. The pavilions had been completed more than fifteen years earlier. Mme de Maintenon wailed: 'What I told the King about Marly did not please him. And yet Marly will soon be a second Versailles.'

She was exaggerating: Marly never was as vast as the other palace; it was rather an unexpected collection of buildings, quite different in structure from all the other royal palaces. That is possibly why Louis XIV loved it so much.

The main stages of its construction are well known: it began with the six pavilions of the wings, those which were meant to flank the central building, which was erected in 1680. Six more pavilions were added in 1684 and 1685. Meanwhile, basins and outhouses were organized, together with the walls and reservoirs. In 1687 the fine watercourse which was to become the Tapis Vert was dug. In 1698 the Trough was built and decorated by Coustou in 1702 with two famous groups. As early as 1686, in fact, the chateau and the gardens had been completed in their general outline. The first magnificent festivity took place there on July 14, 1685, on the occasion of the marriage of the Duc de Bourbon-Condé to Mlle de Nantes, the legitimated daughter born of the love affair of Louise de Vallière and the King.

The Marly architect was Mansart, and the principal decorator Le Brun. As at Versailles, he inspired all the artists who worked there: Coustou, Van der Meulen, Deportes, Ceysevox and others. Le Brun was not always successful in his ideas, and as Pierre de Nolhac justly remarked, the *trompe-l'oeil* painting which covered the outside of the palace often miscarried. Frescoes look better under sunny Italian skies. They are not to be recommended in a damp valley, facing west and constantly exposed to the rain. The constant need of repairs finally got the better of its initial economy. The general idea of the castle is known: the royal pavilion had been erected half-way up the slope: it was the palace of the sun, surrounded on each side with flower beds connected by flowering arbours, and twelve pavilions, six on either side, symbolizing the twelve signs of the zodiac. As nothing is left of these edifices (apart from a few stones on the ground to mark the outline) we must consult the excellent guide book written in 1738 by Piganiol de la Force. The modifications effected after the King's death were, in fact, of little importance. Piganiol entered by the royal gate – still in existence – on the road from Versailles to St Germain. After following a carriage-drive 115 toises long,[1] another gate was passed, the pillars of which were decorated with stone vases sculpted by Coustou. Beyond this lay the forecourt, with a pavilion at either side, the one serving as the chapel and the other as the guard room. In front of them, two more pavilions housed the Court.

The front of the royal pavilion was painted with frescoes and crowned with a pediment sculpted by Jouvenet. Other frescoes covered the façade of the Trophies. Four flights of steps, one on each face, gave access to the interior. Each was adorned with groups of children and sphinxes sculpted by Coustou and Lespingola. The state apartments were reached through vestibules decorated by Van der Meulen and Desportes. The big salon had been decorated with sculptures mostly by Coustou, and paintings by Jouvenet, Coypel, Boulogne le Jeune, etc. Four large apartments opened on the vestibules: those of the King and the Queen (she never came, as it was finished only in the year that she died, and the apartment fell to Mme de Maintenon), Madame, the King's sister-in-law, and the Dauphine. On the ground floor were a smaller drawing-room and a billiards

[1] Nearly 250 yards.

room. The apartments above were reserved exclusively for the princes of the blood.

The twelve pavilions that framed the King's quarters were of one storey and had two windows on each side. They were aligned between the chateau and the Basin. Each of them housed at least two, and possibly four, families of courtiers. The crowding was thus as great as at Versailles, especially as the last two pavilions had been arranged to house two huge globes, one terrestrial, the other celestial, which had been made by Father Coronelli in 1683;[1] they were so big that, from the moment they left Marly, the search for a building in which to show them to the public was continuous but unsuccessful. There is a plan to have them taken to the Petites Ecuries at Versailles. They arrived at Marly in 1703.

In spite of the congestion at Marly, courtiers would have done anything for an opportunity to go there with the King. 'Sire. Sire, Marly!' was a request that became famous. To be singled out was a privilege which was carefully bestowed. It must be admitted that the hospitality there was truly royal. Not only were the guests put to no expense whatever, but each lady found a complete outfit in her room. Servants danced attendance. The guests were attended with as much refinement as their master.

Etiquette was somewhat relaxed at Marly, a fact which shocked the Palatine Princess, Madame being obsessed with ceremonial. As soon as the King had uttered the all-operative sentence: 'Your hats, gentlemen!' you could put on your hat. You were free.

Amusements of every kind, walks, concerts, rural dances and games whiled away the time, and they all did what they pleased. They could follow the King through the gardens while he inspected the groves and supervized the way in which the yew-trees were pruned, like any good landowner, or while he explained his future plans to Mme de Maintenon, or gave instructions for changes to be made to the shape of a basin. They could walk down to the Basin, whence the whole of the estate could be seen and the old town of Marly clinging to the hill; or to the kennels the King had just had built. They could walk back to the big salon to a concert which was about to begin. The King played billiards with Monsieur le Grand Ecuyer or his minister, Chamillart. Supper was served and they all went to bed delighted with his day.

In this sort of life, woven of distractions and of work – for the King met his ministers several times a week – hunting took a prominent part. Forests surrounded the chateau and a short gallop took one into the midst of the thickets. This is why, in the second part of his reign, Louis XIV was so pleased with Marly. He could rest in a setting which was his own creation. As the years elapsed his sojourns became more and more frequent. Crowds of gardeners

[1] An eighteenth century geographer.

maintained the gardens. Their wages rose to 18,000 livres a year, and the King was constantly planning new embellishments. He was at Marly when, on August 10, 1715, he was seized by the sickness which was to kill him three weeks later. He left the royal pavilion never to return.

Marly barely escaped destruction after his death. Cardinal Fleury wanted to do away with the costly building. It was Saint-Simon, the ferocious enemy of Versailles, who saved the chateau. He remarked that 'this fairy palace was unique in all Europe for its form, for the beauty of its fountains, for the reputation given it by the late King; it was one of the sights visited by foreigners of all ranks coming to France'. In 1717 the Czar Peter I visited the chateau.

So Marly was saved. Only the watercourse was transformed into a simple *tapis vert*, because it was too expensive to maintain. Louis XV did not feel for Marly as his great-grandfather had done. He did go there, but not often and not for long. Gambling was fairly heavy at Marly and courtiers were admitted who would not have been tolerated by Louis XIV. The apartments seemed cold and their decoration seemed antiquated. It was the same under Louis XVI. Some thirty guests used to gather round the King or the Queen. Yet the gardens always filled the visitors with admiration. Diderot wrote to Mlle Volland in 1759: 'After dinner, we drifted into the gardens. What struck me was the contrast between the delicate artificiality of the bowers and arbours, and the rustic nature of a thick cluster of tall trees which towers above them and forms a background. It endows the whole landscape with a fairy-like aspect which I find pleasing.'

How, therefore, were those gardens laid out, that so enraptured both Diderot and the Abbé Delille? They should be described as they were before later alterations. They were doubtlessly the work of Le Nôtre, and also Mansart, who was responsible for the bowers and cascades – which was architectural work – and Durusé, who was responsible for certain plantations.

From the upper part of the valley, which adjoined the forest, the 'river' flowed down to the chateau: it was a long cascade enclosed by thickets. Three sea monsters spouted out the water which flowed down fifty-three steps by successive stages and reached a basin decorated with statues of Neptune, Amphitrite, the Seine and the Marne, all done by Coysevox. Walks branched off on either side, leading towards shrubberies and fountains.

This vista, above the central pavilion, was continued through several flower beds decorated with further basins, descending by successive levels to the bottom of the hill, to the Quatre Gerbes basin, the big pool and the Grand Jet, which soared higher than those of Versailles. Each was surrounded with statues by Coustou or Van Cleve. A terrace brought the whole composition to an end. The terrace had a wrought iron balustrade, with decorative groups by Coysevox of Mercury and *Fame riding winged steeds*. These were erected in 1702, taken afterwards to the Tuileries, and replaced by the famous horses which now stand in the Place de la Concorde at the entrance to the Champs Elysées.

70

Near the chateau were graceful green arbours enlivened by numerous pieces of statuary. Below were the 'Green Apartments', truly a sort of vegetable architecture, to use Ernest de Ganay's term – built of thickets and arbours in which vases alternated with statues erected on rocks. Moreover, the shape of those arbours was often altered according to the King's taste, and no royal park had a more transitory décor than Marly.

On either side of the basins, towards the east, stretched the Louvecienne thickets or Bois de la Princesse (after the Duchesse de Bourgogne) with the Amphitheatre of Mercury and the rural waterfall. Other bowers and other basins, connected by small winding walks, had been built down the slope. The Bassin des Muses put the finishing touch to that part of the gardens. A fine painting by Hubert Robert enables us to see what it was like.

When looking at a map of the park, one is struck by the skill with which architects succeeded in making use of the terrain, taking any opportunity without doing violence to nature. Mansart and Le Nôtre displayed a faultless art, which is also found in the so-called Marly thickets situated on the west. It was there that an allegorical group stood that had been acquired in Italy – *Time unveiling the beauty of the arts* as well as Sarazin's *Children playing with a goat*.

To bring water to those fountains and jets, the experts soon made use of the celebrated 'Machine' traditionally ascribed to Rennequin Sualem. It was begun in 1681 and was first meant for raising the Seine water to Versailles. But the park soon acquired its own water supply from a system of ponds and canals, and the 'machine' was used for the Marly gardens, where the water was led up through a great aqueduct of thirty-six arches. All the water poured into the Basin (1702) the supporting wall of which was decorated with shells and rock-work.

What can be seen now of that charming and wonderful composition, of Louis XIV's matchless creation? Only the Tapis Vert, which replaced the watercourse, the Grand Jet and the big basin. One can scarcely find where the lanes, the groves and the other basins were. A low hummock and a few stones mark the site of the King's palace. Two vases by Jouvenet decorate the former royal railing. The Basin is still there, but the vista which Louis XIV could see from the terrace is now obstructed by a railway viaduct.

Yet it was not under the Revolution that the chateau was demolished, but under the Empire. As at Versailles, the Convention had ordered the furniture to be sold, which occupied eighty-seven days and produced the meagre sum of 435,493 livres for the Treasury. Boizot, a sculptor who had been sent by the Fine Arts Commission, had saved the horses, some fifty statues and a dozen paintings. Lead, copper and tin were torn away for war needs: the railings were destroyed to recover the iron, and the groves devastated in the search for lead pipes. In 1799 the estate was sold. A timber merchant bought the clusters of trees. The chateau and park fell for 421,361 francs to an industrialist who set up a cotton mill in the outhouses and a weaving factory in the chateau. He tore to pieces what was left in the way of marble and wrought iron. Finally, in 1808, as his business was doing badly, he had the whole building pulled down, to make some money from the sale of its materials. Two years later, the Imperial household bought back the estate, but by that time the chateau had disappeared and the park was unrecognizable. Only the Basin remained and was acquired by the town of Marly as a public utility. It was restored between the two World Wars.

Today Marly is no more than a memory. Only the Grand Jet, still soaring during the summer months to the delight of visitors, recalls the splendour of the royal park.

South of Paris, between the rustic villages of Fontenay-aux-Roses and Chatenay-Malabry, stretched the town of Sceaux, the parish of which seems to have been separated from that of Chatenay only in the fifteenth century. Its prosperity arose from an estate which in the seventeenth century became one of the finest in the possession of one of Louis XIV's principal officers, Colbert.

Until then the barony of Sceaux had belonged to good families connected with the Paris law courts – Jean Paillard, Councillor to the Parliament of Paris; then Pierre Baillet, Maître des Requêtes in the fifteenth century, whose family kept Sceaux all through the next century. In 1597, the land went to Charlotte Baillet, the Lady of Tresmes, and her husband, Louis Potier, whose descendants, thanks to astute purchases, finally assumed the title of Duc de Tresmes.

Hitherto this dwelling had been no more than a good bourgeois family home. Louis Potier had the first chateau built. His younger son, René, whose elder brother had been killed at the siege of Montauban in 1621, succeeded in getting his estate turned into a barony. He died in 1670 when ninety-one, and his heirs sold Sceaux to Colbert for 135,000 livres. Colbert gradually enlarged the estate and altered and enlarged the chateau. It is likely that his architect was Charles Perrault, and almost certain that Le Nôtre designed his gardens. All the great artists who had worked at Versailles were bent on embellishing the chateau of the Superintendent of Buildings, a great patron of the arts. Secondary buildings were erected, some of which are still standing, and the Petit Château, near the village, completed the estate, the decoration of which was in 1677 sufficiently complete for the Minister to invite the King as his guest. Louis XIV was present at a performance of *Phèdre*.

Jean-Baptiste Colbert, Marquis de Seignelay, in 1683 inherited his father's enormous fortune and his office of Secretary of State for the Navy. He continued the work on the chateau and commissioned Hardouin-Mansart to build the orangery, had the Grand Canal dug, had the Grand Parterre designed and accumulated works of arts inside the chateau. In 1685, he entertained the King to a fête, the splendour of which was never forgotten. The *Idylle de Sceaux* was written by Racine and Lulli for that very occasion.

Seignelay died in 1690. His lavishness had seriously depleted his fortune. Gaps had to be filled. In 1699 the Sceaux estate was sold for more than a million livres to the Duc du Maine, the legitimated son of Louis XIV and Athénais de Rochechouart-Mortemart, Marquise de Montespan.

The Duke was then twenty-seven years of age. In 1693 he had married Louise Bénédicte de Bourbon-Condé, granddaughter of the victor of Rocroi. She was on bad terms with Mme de Maintenon at Versailles and was therefore delighted to have her own chateau. According to the Palatine Princess, who was lacking, it is true, in generosity, she was no beauty, but she was vivacious, lively and witty. Sceaux became a select place, which she made a rendezvous for wits and writers who have not always been remembered by posterity. There was Nicolas de Malezieux (mathematician, poet and writer of operas), President Hénault (who relapsed into piety too late), Saint-Aulaire (member of the French Academy; no one knows why) and Fontenelle, the best-known of all.

While Versailles was sinking into etiquette and boredom under the austere rule of the lady who had founded St Cyr, Sceaux formed a contrast, and its nocturnal festivities were alive with illuminations, games and spectacles.

The *Nuits de Sceaux*, which took place in 1714 and 1715, remained famous. Rose Delaunay, who later became Mme de Stael, has described them, and it is through her, who played a big part, that we have today an account of those allegorical presentations in which Night took its revenge on Day. This was a clear hint at the opposition between Sceaux and Versailles: Night triumphant (and hoping for an even greater triumph) and Day declining.

For the Duchess of Maine (Ludovise, as her intimate friends called her) was dreaming of future power. Under a frivolous air she hid a formidable ambition. It is difficult to know how far she went, from a sentimental point of view; she has been ascribed more lovers than she probably had. On the other hand, she knew that in his will Louis XIV had bequeathed his power to his favourite son. She was horribly disappointed when, after the King's death, the will was declared illegal. Three years later, under the influence of a triumphant aristocracy, her husband was deprived of his offices and of his title of Prince of the Blood. That was more than the Duchess could bear: hoping for revenge, and against her husband's wish, she threw herself into a conspiracy organized by the Spanish Ambassador, Count Cellamare.

What followed is well known: the plot was discovered. Several of the Duchess' friends, who had participated in the intrigue out of devotion, were arrested. The Duke was taken to the fortress of Doullens, the Duchess to Dijon, and the rest exiled or sent to the Bastille.

All was soon forgotten. A year later the Duchess returned to her beloved chateau at Sceaux, forgiven by her husband. But henceforth her receptions were more discreet. Mythological comedies, in which Ludovise had displayed so much talent, were superceded by the pleasures of the table. Such pleasures were less noisy.

The Duke died in 1736; poets and friends disappeared one after the other. Of course, there were new faces. It is said that Voltaire, who had taken refuge at Sceaux after some peccadillo, wrote *Zadig* there. In her turn, the Duchess died in Paris in 1753: she was seventy-seven and belonged to another age. Her eldest son, the Prince des Dombes, inherited Sceaux and died two years later. The estate went to his brother, who had lived there quietly and retired. When he died, Sceaux went to the Duc de Penthièvre, Louis XIV's grandson through his father, the Comte de Toulouse, the Duc du Maine's brother: we have already met him elsewhere.

He did not come often to Sceaux. He housed Florian there, who wrote some of his works in the park, and after he had been elected to the French Academy gave a reception for that illustrious body at Sceaux. Earlier, in 1677, Colbert had received the Academy in the Pavillon de l'Aurore. History was repeating itself after 110 years.

Times had changed. In 1789 the Duc de Penthièvre gave Sceaux to his daughter, the Duchess of Orleans. Philippe-Egalité's wife came seldom. When she was arrested during the Revolution, Sceaux was confiscated and a school of agriculture was established there. As at Marly, the roofs were deprived of their lead. The library and the works of art were dispersed, but not all were destroyed. A part of the gardens (the Menagerie) was sold in 1798. What was left was sold to a St Malo merchant, Lecomte, who looted the whole thing and razed it to the ground. In 1831 nothing but the chapel survived. It served as a workshop and disappeared in its turn for lack of maintenance.

Under the Second Empire, the Marquis de Trevise, who had married Lecomte's daughter, tried to repair the estate. He was fairly successful in restoring Le Nôtres fine vistas. He was less successful when building a pseudo-Louis XIII chateau to replace its predecessor. Its cramped, graceless lines do not harmonise with the beautiful surrounding framework.

There were further festivities at Sceaux up to the first World War, but the estate was less and less cared for and was in danger of falling into the hands of developers. It was saved by the Seine Department, which bought it in 1923. A small part of it was actually sold, in an intelligent way, in order to find the money necessary for restoration. As the chateau has now been turned into a *Musée de l'Ile-de-France*, after having been badly treated by the Germans during the last war, it is now out of danger.

When walking in the park, one is impressed by the majesty and dignity of Le Nôtre's imagination. The gardener of Versailles was faced with the difficult problem presented by a steeply sloping terrain. Instead of minimizing the slopes, he increased them. The terrain was vast and, according to a plan which he held dear, he created long perspectives. One axis cut by the chateau comprised a long ceremonial drive forming the entrance and continuing beyond the building through flower beds, to disappear in the distance beyond Antony. It was about a mile and a quarter long and it made a long Tapis Vert, flower beds and basins possible along a gentle slope. On the right of the chateau on the Sceaux side, bowers and flower beds were most skilfully designed. They were separated by secondary paths of a rather fanciful design, for Le Nôtre never sought absolute symmetry. Below those groves were the kitchen garden and the poultry yard. The Pavilion de l'Aurore stands in the centre of the former kitchen garden.

This pavilion was put up by Perrault at the same time as the chateau. It is a rotunda with an elegantly rounded dome, flanked by two small wings. The interior contains a big painting by Le Brun which explains the name of the pavilion: Aurora leaves Inferno and, putting the Night to flight, heralds the arrival of Apollo. The painting was a tactful compliment from Colbert to Louis XIV. Under this dome the members of the Academy were received and treated to a speech of six-hundred lines in verse by Quinault, which left them the time to admire Le Brun's masterpiece, the subject of the fullsome poem. The paintings in the two rooms in the wings were done by Delobel and were only put there in 1752.

The great transverse axis crossed the first at the level of the chateau. It comprised the Allée de la Duchesse, which passed through the woods to reach the Grande Cascade, the waters of which pour into the wide Octagon basin. This axis continued beyond, up into the woods on the other side. A parallel line to the first was formed by the Grand Canal, the middle of which is a basin connected by a short waterway to the Octagon basin.

All this was not built at once. The Grand Canal was dug in the time of Seignelay and it must be looked at from the Guinea Hen Terrace. This fine waterlane, long abandoned, has now recovered all its dignity and the double line of poplars along its banks provide the most majestic of frameworks.

To the end of the secondary axis formed by the Octagon basin, its connecting link with the Canal and the Dahlia Garden, was brought in 1930 the so-called Pavillon de Hanovre, built by Chevotet for Marshal de Richelieu. It was given this nickname by the Parisians, who claimed that it had been paid for by the prodigious loot Richelieu had brought back from the German campaign. Threatened with destruction, it has been skilfully rebuilt in the park.

The waterfalls were completely rebuilt during the last century. Nothing remained of those designed by Le Brun and decorated by Coysevox, Girardon and their pupils. The present waterfalls, with their buffet, the Rodin masks from which the water spouts, and the stair-like basins form a rather heavy composition. They must be seen when they are covered with streaming water pouring into the Octagon basin. The latter, built by Le Nôtre, is enlivened like the Grand

Canal by swans that glide slowly over its mirroring water. The many fishermen who surround the Octagon do not deprive the scene of its rural aspect.

On the left of the chateau rises the orangery which Mansart built between 1683 and 1685. It shelters the orange trees which during the summer adorn the flower beds; it is also used as a lecture-room and music-room for the Ile de France Museum. In spite of the destruction of one of the pavilions that flank the nave the building is still quite harmonious. Together with the Pavillon de l'Aurore and the Petit Château (built at the beginning of the seventeenth century and added by Colbert to his estate) it provides the most interesting evidence of the old buildings.

Indeed, to get some idea of these, one must look at the prints preserved in the museum. The chateau was on severe lines, fitting marvellously well into the landscape. A central pavilion with two wings and two more pavilions completed the buildings. There was a first floor and a second one with only small rectangular windows. Sculpted frontons, and statues between the windows, decorated the façades, the simplicity of which contrasted with the splendour of the gardens.

Though the chateau has disappeared, the gardens are luckily recovering their former splendour. Sceaux is still one of the finest examples of Le Nôtre's genius, and stands at the very gates of Paris.

Though it never belonged to a reigning family under the Old Régime, Chantilly is none the less a royal castle, which in the seventeenth century was compared with Versailles. It is true that the ostentation of the Condés, and the sumptuousness of their festivities and receptions, equalled those of the Sun-King, their cousin.

By an ironical stroke of fate the estate fell into the hands of the Duc d'Aumale, Louis-Philippe's son, in 1830; but eighteen years later, the Orleans ceased to reign over France and, after having rebuilt the Grand Château which had been destroyed during the Revolution, the Duke bequeathed Chantilly to the Institut de France, which cares assiduously for the treasures he collected.

Was *Cantiliacus* the Gallo-Roman villa of a landowner named Cantilius? It is quite likely. As a fief, surrounded by forests in the Nonette valley, it is not mentioned before the twelfth century. It was on a group of rocks thrusting out above the marshes that the first owners built their fortress; they were a local family called Bouteiller, after their function at the court of the King of France. They had to fight hard against their neighbours, the powerful abbey of St Denis, and the priory of Chalais, which was connected with St Leu-d'Esserent. In 1358, the fortress was looted by peasants in revolt during the Jacquerie, caused partly by the misfortunes of the Anglo-French wars; it was most unpropitious for Guillaume le Bouteiller, whose fortune was already deteriorating. Finally, the castle was bought by Pierre d'Orgemont in 1386. He became Charles VI's chancellor. He enlarged his estate, buying Vineul, St Firmin and Quincampoix (now spelt Quinquempoix). On the same site, well surrounded by marshes and ponds which were being impounded, the castle was rebuilt between 1388 and 1394 in the shape of an irregular quadrilateral. With its fortified forecourt, surrounded by broad moats and flanked with seven towers, it formed a powerful stronghold within which the Orgemont family could safely amass its treasures.

The castle was captured by the Anglo-Burgundians and reconquered by Charles VI's army. It did not suffer much damage and was not altered during the fifteenth century.

About 1450, Marguerite d'Orgemont, Pierre's descendant, married Jean II de Montmorency and brought the castle into that powerful family. Henceforth, the destiny of Chantilly was sealed.

From the time when they gave Blanche de Castille a wise councillor, the Montmorencys had always been seen on the King's battlefields or in his entourage. The family was rich and powerful. Yet it was neither Jean II de Montmorency nor his son Guillaume who undertook the reconstruction of Chantilly, but their descendant, Marguerite d'Orgemont's grandson Anne, the future Constable of France. He became proprietor of the estate from 1522. As early as 1524 he created a garden west of the chateau and ordered large consignments of plum, cherry and mulberry trees from Languedoc and Normandy. The garden ended in a gallery above the meadow of Bucamp. Anne went to Italy with Francis I. The works at Chantilly, which were temporarily suspended, were resumed when he returned. Martin de Meilles painted life-like stags in the gallery and the walls were decorated with their antlers. In front of the gallery the flower beds were laid out in a chequered fashion.

In 1527 Anne de Montmorency married Madeleine of Savoy. Major alterations then began. The general layout was retained: the keep, into which new windows were opened, the external ramparts with their towers and *chemin-de-ronde*, remained; but the curtain walls were topped with one or two more stories. The whole east wing, which formed the main body of the mansion, and the right wing, containing superimposed galleries, were rebuilt. Pierre I de Chambiges was the originator of that magnificent work; his inspiration was the school of the Loire. At the entrance a flight of steps, covered by a porch and a bell-turret, formed a strikingly elegant outwork. Anne de Montmorency collected works of art in his new castle. He entertained Charles V of Spain, who expressed his admiration by proclaiming that Chantilly was the equal of the most splendid among the royal chateaux. Rabelais thought so too. To praise the beauty of his imaginary Abbey de Thélème, he compared it to Chantilly.

But Anne de Montmorency was not yet satisfied. Lower than the rock of Chantilly and beside it was a small island. About 1558, the Constable decided to have a small castle built there. His architect was Jean Bullant, Comptroller of the King's Buildings, with Pierre Desilles as contractor. Built after the style of antique Italian monuments, it was completed a few years before the Constable's death. Its external aspect has not changed much and we can still contemplate its façades, which were skilfully planned to avoid any monotony: sunk deep into the capital, the dormer-windows break the straight line. The checkered disposition of doors and windows on the inner façade, the elegance of the corinthian columns on either side of the main entrance, stress the part played by an architect who could successfully combine sobriety and perfection.

Anne de Montmorency died in 1567; his sons, François and Henri, were equally enamoured with Chantilly. Festivities were frequent and chosen guests found faultless hospitality there. Henri de Montmorency was made Constable in 1595 and gave a magnificent reception in honour of Henri IV. But the Vert-Galant repaid him poorly. At the end of his reign he fell madly in love with Henri de Montmorency's daughter, the charming Charlotte who had married Henri II, Prince de Condé. The latter had to flee from Chantilly and from France to protect his wife. Ravaillac's knife put an end to this comedy.

The last Duc de Montmorency, also named Henri, was Marshal of France under Louis XIII and his fate was tragic. Ostentatious and gay, he displayed a magnificence which astonished his contemporaries. He was broadminded and he patronized even libertine writers. Theophile de Viau,[1] threatened with imprisonment in 1623 for publishing erotic verses that had been condemned by Parliament, took refuge at Chantilly. He was the one who gave the name Sylvie to Montmorency's wife, Marie-Félicité des Ursins, whom he adored. The small house, now named Sylvie's House, was built for her brother-in-law, François. Refinement and affectation, luxury and courage, went hand-in-hand with political ambition, thrusting Henri de Montmorency into plotting with Gaston d'Orléans, the King's brother. The plot was discovered, Richelieu was merciless and the last Duc de Montmorency was beheaded in Toulouse in 1632.

The chateau was confiscated. Louis XIII took the opportunity to go there often to hunt. It has even been said that he appropriated and took to the house some of the artistic treasures which had been brought together by the Montmorencys. Yet princes could forgive. Anne of Austria restored Chantilly to Charlotte de Montmorency, the luckless duke's sister, in 1643. Charlotte was the Duc d'Enghien's mother. The Grand Condé had just been victorious at Rocroi: it was difficult to remain resentful towards a family that had fought so well.

With the Grand Condé, Chantilly entered a new period of opulence. The poets of the Hôtel de Rambouillet flocked back to Chantilly. Mme de Scudéry painted the portrait of the owner as Cyrus, and the court of Chantilly compared proudly with that of St Germain. But the example of Henri de Montmorency's death was of no avail. The Grand Condé threw himself into the Fronde, under the influence of his sister the Duchesse de Longueville. He ended by betraying

---

[1] French lyrical poet and dramatist (1590-1625).

France and passed over to the Spaniards. Once more, in its owner's absence, Chantilly became a royal residence. When Christina of Sweden visited France, she was received by Louis XIV and Monsieur at Chantilly. With the Peace of the Pyrenees Condé was given a contemptuous pardon by the King and allowed to return to France. A few years later he was even permitted to return to Chantilly. Thanks to his major-domo Gourville, the chateau had not suffered from its long desertion. Condé thenceforth devoted himself to gardening. Le Nôtre and La Quintinie, politely lent by Louis XIV, transformed the terrain, cut long avenues across the forest and created flower beds which were enlivened by fountains. Though done on a very large scale, the work was complete in a few years, and in 1671 Condé invited Louis XIV to a most dazzling reception.

Mme de Sévigné, that tireless letter-writer, described those unforgettable days to her daughter: 'The King arrived at Chantilly last night,' she wrote. 'He hunted a stag by moonlight. The lanterns did wonders. The firework display looked wan, rather dimmed by the light of our friend the moon. But anyway, the evening, the supper, the gaming, were all marvellous. . . .'

Alas! the delight was clouded by the suicide of Vatel. The Prince's cook, over-wrought and exhausted by twelve sleepless nights, lost his head when he was told by mistake that the fish had not arrived and ran himself through with his sword. Louis XIV was much affected and asked to be more simply entertained thereafter. But that did not bring poor Vatel back to life, Mme de Sévigné concluded.

While remaining henceforth perfectly loyal to the King, Condé had brought a true court together at Chantilly. The wits flocked back. Writers loved the place. La Bruyére met Boussuet there and loved to stroll along those 'splendid lanes to the sound of those gushing waters that never cease, day or night'. Racine and Boileau often joined them. The Prince took them under his protection, which at times was rather heavy. Condé could not bear to be contradicted. Following a long discussion with Boileau, the latter concluded by saying: 'Henceforth, my Lord, I shall always agree with you when you are wrong.'

Meanwhile, the Montmorency's Grand Château, in spite of many alterations, seemed out of date. A short time before his death, Condé ordered Mansart to rebuild it. After the Prince's death, the work was carried on by his son Henri-Jules. On the very same spot a majestic building arose, flanked with towers and crowned with a dome. A new entrance replaced the fortified courtyard. Apart from the foundations, practically nothing was left of Pierre de Chambiges' work. On the other hand, the Petit Château was preserved but completely re-organized inside. Sauveur Lecomte celebrated Condé's victories in a set of large panels. A menagery was organized in the park. Mansart rebuilt Sylvie's house, which Le Nôtre surrounded with groves and flower beds.

Henri-Jules definitely made Chantilly the family residence. His son, the Duc de Bourbon, was Louis XV's Prime Minister after the Law débacle. For his own part, Louis-Henri de Bourbon had lost nothing by Law's system. It was even said that he had trebled his fortune. He kept Chantilly on a regal footing, surrounded by his friends and his mistress, the Marquise de Prie. He entertained Louis XV there, who hunted in the forest.

For hunting was still the main, the usual distraction for Chantilly's guests. That was doubtless why Henri de Condé had his splendid stables built by Jean Aubert between 1719 and 1740. The Duc de Bourbon even thought of rebuilding the chateau yet again, but he had not the time. Anyway, the Petit Château was decorated by splendid panellings in the best taste of the period, and near the Grande Galerie Huet painted the so-called Salon des Singes.

The last Condé but one, the Duc d'Enghien's grandfather, was another pleasant and witty prince. He had the Château d'Enghien built for his grandson near the entrance to the terrace which is majestically decorated with a statue of the Constable, who seems to welcome the visitors. Before Marie-Antoinette he conceived the fashionable idea of erecting light and rustic buildings in the park, the Hameau or hamlet, where rural fêtes were presented. The 'English' garden surrounded them, where one could sail on the Grand Canal in the little boats gathered in a tiny harbour. Comedies or operas by Favart, Grétry or Sedaine were performed in the new theatre built by Louis Joseph de Condé in 1767. Such were the sumptuous but refined pleasures of a society that was very soon to vanish.

In 1788 the Condés were among the first to leave France. The castle was confiscated and stripped of its furniture. It was turned into a prison. The forest had become national property. Several parts of the park had been broken up. Finally, the castle was handed over for demolition and razed to the level of the terrace. There was no time to destroy the Petit Château. The stables were used as barracks by a cavalry regiment; they survived, as did the Hameau and Sylvie's House.

Yet Chantilly was in a pitiful state when it was restored to the Condés after the Restoration. When Czar Alexander paid a visit there he had to open an umbrella while walking in the gallery of the Petit Château. After the Prince's death in 1818 his son undertook the first work of restoration. He had the canals cleaned, some flower beds reorganized and he made what was left habitable. He bequeathed the estate to Louis-Philippe's son the Duc d'Aumale, who took possession in 1830.

By 1840 the latter began to restore Chantilly to its early grandeur, but the revolution of 1848 interrupted the work. When in 1872, on Thiers suggestion, the National Assembly restored the Duke's property, he went on with his former plans. Between 1876 and 1882 Daumet completely rebuilt the Grand Château, which was destined to house the dazzling art collections of that illustrious patron.

In 1886 the Duke bequeathed Chantilly to the Institute of France, which took

possession of it at his death in 1897. During the first world war the castle was for several years the French G.H.Q.

Of the older structure nothing remains today but the Petit Chateau or Capitainerie, now closely united to the Grand Chateau, the Grandes Ecuries (stables), the Château d'Enghien, the Caboutière and Sylvie's House, the Hameau, the tennis court and St Paul's chapel, one of the seven chapels built by the Constable in the park in the middle of the sixteenth century to commemorate the seven stations of Rome, where he had been on pilgrimage. The modern castle is a careful reproduction of the one built by Mansart, and the furniture, the tapestries and the works of art to be seen there make one easily forget the rather weighty appearance of the building. It fits well with the Capitainerie, and the pointed roofs, the turrets and the domes mirror themselves in the surrounding waters.

On the edge of the racecouse the stables raise their impressive façade. It has been said that they may be the finest example of the civil architecture of the eighteenth century. It was difficult, in such a functional building, to blend so much grandeur and harmony. The great horses sculpted on the tympanum of the entrance, the open arcades of the riding school, the fountain in the central rotunda – everything unites in a monument worthy of the Louvre or Versailles. It is easy to understand why Paul I, dining in this building at Chantilly, of which he knew nothing, thought he was in 'the most splendid drawing-room in the palace', and was rather staggered when the curtains were drawn aside and he saw the horses in their stalls.

The park – or what is left of the original design – was one of Le Nôtre's masterpieces. Instead of setting the gardens on the axis of one or other of the entrances to the Grand Château, he set them on either side of the terrace and the Constable's statue, which since 1612 has stood in the centre.

On one side one reaches the French Garden by a straight flight of steps with secondary flights on either side: this is the Grand Degré, decorated with statues of the rivers and of mythological characters, sculpted by Hardy in 1684 after Le Nôtre's drawings. Directly in front is the Grande Gerbe and beyond it the Grand Parterre, the geometrical balance of which has great dignity. The Grand Canal, fed by the waters of the Nonette, stretches down to the Parterre and for a mile and a quarter beyond. It is easy to imagine the Grand Condé there, with Boussuet and La Bruyère in endless discussion. . . . On the other bank of the Canal (which extends as far as the Canardière) the Vertugadin lawn closes the view with a statue of Diana the Huntress in the middle.

Let us return to the terrace. As early as 1663, Le Nôtre and his nephew Claude Desgots had laid out the western flower bed, which became that of the Orangery when the latter was built by Mansart between 1682 and 1686. Further on, the secondary canals formed islands which were named the Ile d'Amour and Ile du Bois-Vert. This part of the park was embellished with thickets and waterfalls, the water of which flowed into basins. Only vestiges remain: here Cupid's statue still watches over the Ile d'Amour, where of the Temple of Venus only a few columns remain. An 'English' garden was laid out there in 1820, in the part of the garden that had been destroyed by the Revolution.

Like Versailles, St Cloud and most of the royal residences, Chantilly was a continuous creation. The Grand Condé's son erected more statues in the formal garden. Nicolas Breteuil continued Le Nôtre's work. It is to him we owe the Temple of Venus, round which the Princes' visitors used to indulge in amorous play and in games of skill, amused themselves with the swings or played at nine-holes. In 1770 a maze was built in Sylvie's groves, and a Chinese kiosk too, in pursuit of fashion. Fifteen years later, the old Stag Gallery of the Montmorencys was pulled down and a terrace erected instead.

All these alterations did not rob the park of its charm. Chantilly is undoubtedly one of the finest museums in France; the paintings by Poussin, Memling and Clouet, collected by the Duc d'Aumale, together with priceless manuscripts, tapestries, sculptures and so on, are staggering. The chapel (rebuilt in 1882 where the old one had stood) still has panels and stained-glass windows from the Renaissance, an altar by Jean Goujon and Bullant, the impressive mausoleum of Henri II of Bourbon-Condé, carved by Jacques Sarazin. Chantilly is the gorgeous setting for collections patiently got together by a patron of great taste.

Yet lovers, hands entwined, prefer perhaps to wander in Sylvie's glades, or beside the pond, or under the forest leaves, more interested in each other than in the splendid scene that surrounds them.

CHAPTER IV

THE EIGHTEENTH CENTURY

THE age of the great royal buildings ended with the reign of Louis XIV. Of course, in the eighteenth century the talent of the architects did not decline, and for the new tastes which the Marquise de Pompadour and her friends imposed during the reign of Louis XV they contrived original and elegant edifices. But no more vast palaces arose, and the delightful houses left to us by a century of refined living – so far as they survive – were meant rather to shelter a King's amours or his mistresses' pleasures than to entertain a whole court: Bagatelle, Bellevue, Louveciennes are the most characteristic examples of the period.

Others, like Rambouillet or Choisy, were much older. But they became royal property in the eighteenth century and then were altered so much that they may be justly included with the rest.

Rambouillet, for instance, entered history in the eighth century! At the beginning of the Middle Ages almost the whole forest of Yvelines belonged to the Abbey of St Denis. A fief belonging to this abbey, a village of some twenty dwellings, inhabited by woodcutters and clogmakers: such was Rambouillet at that time. Under Charles V it was bought by a former provost of Paris, Jean Bernier, who within six years erected a very simple fortified house there, of two main buildings at right-angles, with turrets at their extremities. To the north stood a fortified gate behind a bridge which served to prohibit access to the castle, which was protected by a large round tower, connected by curtain walls to the main building and the gate. The neighbouring marshes brought water to the moat that lay at the foot of the walls. The whole building was austere: fourteenth century architecture was essentially military. There was one big vaulted hall, lit by three large bays, and two smaller rooms. Such was the structure of the castle of Rambouillet, which all the architects respected, and which explains its present aspect.

Jean Bernier entertained Charles VI and Philip of Burgundy at his castle on April 9, 1383. This was the first royal visit, and there were to be others. But his son, Guillaume, did not like Rambouillet and early in the fifteenth century he sold the fief to Reynault d'Angennes, the King's Chamberlain who came of an old family of the Drouais. On three different occasions English troops besieged the castle (which was captured and recaptured) and battered its walls. In the sixteenth century, Rabelais was entertained there by Jacques d'Angennes; he compared a nearby rock to a cooking pot, and that rock has accordingly been given the name of the author of *Gargantua*. Later, a grave event took place at Rambouillet. After hunting in the Yvelines forest, Francis I felt unwell and plague was suspected. He was put into quarantine in the west tower and he died there on March 31, 1547. Henceforth the tower was known as Francis I's Tower, and was respectfully preserved, alongside more recent buildings. At least, such is the tradition, and a good number of historians accept it as reliable. To enlarge his castle, Jacques d'Angennes got a local architect, Ymbert, to build a gallery on the ground floor: it still survives. He entertained Francis II and Mary Queen of Scots (1559) there, and Catherine de Medici who was told at Rambouillet the result of the battle at Dreux between Catholics and Huguenots. Henri III also came to Rambouillet when escaping from his rebellious capital, and so did Henri IV in 1598. Nicolas d'Angennes was then lord of the manor.

His son Charles induced Louis XIII, who hunted in the forest, to turn the estate into a marquisate. But he and his wife Catherine, the divine Marquise de Rambouillet, preferred their Paris house, near the Louvre, to this feudal domain. Mme de Rambouillet, the queen of the *Precieuses*, surrounded by her court of admirers, wits, beaus and poets, liked better to dally in more sentimental alleys than in those of her rustic chateau. Yet, together with her daughter Julie she sometimes took the whole party there, where they played games of questionable taste. Finally, Julie married Montausier, who had been her suitor for almost twenty years; he had served as the model for Molière's *Misanthrope* but it seems that it was quite a happy marriage. He survived his wife for nine years and died in 1690. Their daughter married the Duc de Crussol d'Uzés and herself died in 1695, so heavily in debt that the castle had to be sold in 1700 for 140,000 livres to Jean-Baptiste Fleuriau, the lord of Armenonville.

This former Intendant of Finances was the real creator of the park that encircles the chateau. He had the marshes that stretched eastwards drained and a first canal, which had been begun by Montausier, was dug. It flowed in front of the chateau and divided into several smaller branches to form a trapeze-like figure at the top and bottom of which several secondary canals ended. At the ends of the lateral branches, which formed a V, were the Ile des Festins and the Ile des Roches. At either end of the original canal a basin was dug, to the east the Rondeau and to the west the Miroir. This system of waterways of unusual size was completed within a few years. The parterre was then laid out and decorated with mythological marbles, depicting Alpheus, Arethusa or Latona, and terminal statues on pedestals bordered the terrace. Flower beds and lawns increasingly adorned the park.

Fleuriau d'Armenonville did not long enjoy the wonders he had created, which were compared to those of Versailles or Marly by rather flattering contemporaries. The Comte de Toulouse, a son of Louis XIV and Mme de Montespan, hinted that he would like to own such a fine estate. Fleuriau was too tactful not to defer at once to the Prince's wish . . . in return for half a million livres and the Captaincy of the Bois de Boulogne, in which this tireless builder immediately erected a hunting lodge which still bears his name.

The Comte de Toulouse started altering the chateau, which has been left untouched by Fleuriau as he was far too busy with the gardens. The medieval walls were kept, but the east wing was doubled to put in new apartments. The great west halls were set aside for the King and his court. A semi-circular vestibule was built into the angle of the two buildings, giving a rectangular appearance to the courtyard. All the façades were given a classical layout. Finally, a gateway connected the Francis I Tower to the one above the entrance. Under the supervision of Robert de Cotte, the new architect, Sarda, displayed a splendid ingenuity.

The King came to Rambouillet when the work was completed in August 1707. He praised this elegant structure and came to hunt there on several occasions. In spite of the many courtiers, for the court always followed the King, everybody was delighted with the charming gardens and the beautiful receptions. Dangeau wrote that 'the more the King saw the country round Rambouillet, the more he liked it'.

After his marriage with the charming Sophie de Noailles the Comte de Toulouse decided to enlarge the chateau even further. This time he set to work on the west. The turret was taken off and the wing was enlarged by the construction of the 'Assembly' buildings, having oak woodwork of indescribable elegance and richness. It is really like lacework, carved out of a material which has been given back its original hue, endowing it with a delicate grace. Yet a background of gilded wood had to be rubbed off, robbing it of some of its splendour. A little later, the Comte de Toulouse had these apartments extended to the Francis I Tower, which was now connected to the three other rooms thus formed. The identical decoration of these rooms quite dazzled the Comte's guests. The gardens were not overlooked: the canals – especially those which formed a star-like pattern – were completed, flower beds were altered and new statues were put up.

Louis XV, like his great-grandfather, liked Rambouillet. He also liked the Comtesse de Toulouse, a charitable, lively, witty woman. After her husband's death, the King continued to hunt in the forest of Yvelines. He heaped benefits and favours on the son of the deceased, the Duc de Penthièvre, and the chateau became a secret rendezvous for his love affairs with the Mmes de Mailly and de Vintimille, and later Mme de Chateauroux, who were three sisters. The Duc de Penthièvre, Toulouse's son, was unmarried and he gladly lent Rambouillet to his royal nephew. Yet Mme de Pompadour did not come there often. The Duke had by now married the Duke of Modena's daughter, who gave him seven children, of whom only two survived, Mlle de Penthièvre, who became Duchess of Orleans, and the Duc de Lamballe. Then she died in 1754 and the inconsolable duke devoted himself to his high offices at court, the care of his large estates and charitable works. Without neglecting his duties at Versailles, the prince, one of the most noble of eighteenth century characters, preferred to live at Rambouillet. The Princesse de Lamballe, widowed quite early, had an English garden built for her between the Tapis Vert and the Chartres road, complete with little structures like the Shell Pavilion. Garlands, baskets of flowers and fruit, cornices, pilasters – anything in fact – were made of shells. This was the last the Penthièvres did at Rambouillet.

For in fact, Louis XVI, a keen huntsman, wanted a chateau close to the forest through which he often rode. He did not like the one at St Hubert much, where his grandfather had come with his mistresses. He made the Duc de Penthièvre understand that Rambouillet would suit him admirably. That is how, in January 1784, the old Bernier and Angennes home came into royal possession at the cost of sixteen million livres.

Marie-Antoinette is supposed to have said that the chateau was 'a Gothic toadhole', and to make it more comfortable, the King asked the Comte d'Angiviller, just appointed 'Governor of the castle, parks, woods and estate of Rambouillet', to alter what was necessary, while Hubert Robert was given the task of making the gardens conform to contemporary taste. He hastened to lay out little green arbours, all different, but all contrived of fruit trees all of one kind. He planted acacias. Above all, he created the dairy and its garden.

The Queen's Dairy was a lovely pavilion built by Thévenon between 1785 and 1787. It consisted of two rooms, one of which was a rotunda, a marble room decorated with vases, the other a square one, opening on a grotto where water trickled. There the sculptor put the delightful group of the *Girl with a goat*, now in the Louvre, and bas-reliefs which are now dispersed.

As for the chateau proper, it was not altered much. Louis XVI took the west wing for himself, Marie-Antoinette the east. On the other hand, the outhouses were much enlarged and stables were built. Angiviller organized along the edge of the park the model farm and the sheep-fold for which a flock of merinos was ordered from Spain and became one of the glories of Rambouillet.

Louis XVI was planning to have the chateau pulled down and a modern one erected instead; plans were being prepared when the Revolution broke out. The estate was confiscated, the furniture sold, and the park rented out. The story was the same at all the royal estates. Rambouillet was abandoned but did not suffer too much. Prisoners were crowded into the new buildings. Then the chateau passed into Napoleon's hands; he asked the architect Trepsat to restore it, for he had decided to use it as a hunting lodge.

Trepsat set to work. He began by pulling down the west wing, so beautifully laid out by the Comte de Toulouse, and the old fortified gate; he replaced the fine entrance portico, which was no longer in the middle of the façade, by a heavy postern. He rebuilt the east turret and filled the Mirror basin with the rubble. None of this improved the external appearance of the chateau, but Napoleon said he was pleased with the result. Several rooms were arranged for him in the 'Assembly' apartments, adjoining the Francis I Tower; here the decorations have been preserved in part, especially his bathroom. After his marriage to Marie-Louise he had a long balcony built along the whole of the park façade so that he could slip unnoticed into the Empress' apartments. The park recovered its former splendour. The canals were cleaned. Swans enlivened the basins. The islands, mere meadows until then, were planted with trees.

Napoleon stayed several times at Rambouillet. In 1814 the chateau gave shelter to the fugitive Marie-Louise and the King of Rome, who owned a palace in the town (the former Angiviller mansion) but never occupied it. It was at Rambouillet that the Emperor of Austria joined his daughter. After the disaster of Waterloo, it was Napoleon himself who took refuge at the chateau. He left on June 30th in the morning. Blücher and his Prussians occupied the place and did not respect it.

Under Louis XVIII, Rambouillet resumed its traditional role. A last alteration was made. The architect Famin started to rebuild the south front, the only part of Jacques d'Angennes' chateau which had so far been spared. In the axis of the Grand Canal and the Tapis Vert, he erected in 1820 a new front between the south and west turrets. Work was suspended before they were completed so that the heavy and graceless bays of the big salon are not at the centre of the composition. The south turret, which was to disappear, was spared.

It seems to have been the fate of Rambouillet to give refuge to fugitive sovercigns. After Marie-Louise and Napoleon came Charles X, escaping from his rebellious capital. With his family he spent four days at Rambouillet. On the evening of August 3, 1830, they took the road of exile, fearing the approach of a revolutionary army, which, however, had been reduced to a few hundred young men.

Louis-Philippe excluded Rambouillet from the civil list. The hunting-lodge and the chateau were rented first of all to Baron Schickler, and later to Comte Duchatel. The latter gave it up in 1849 and a new tenant was vainly sought. Then everyone became resigned to the idea of pulling the chateau down, but it was finally saved by the railway. Rambouillet became one of the main outings for Parisians in search of fresh air. Holiday trains were organized as early as 1851: for two-francs-fifty it was possible to spend a whole day in the park and forest. A funfair was organized, and for a time there was a restaurant in the chateau.

Nevertheless, its destiny remained unsettled. Napoleon III saved it. He did not stay there, but he hunted in the forest with illustrious guests. After the fall of the Second Empire, the Duc de la Tremouille rented the chateau, but since

1883 it has been maintained for the Presidents of the Republic. Some of them stayed there in the summer, while others merely brought guests there to hunt. Government guests are often entertained there.

Thus the least splendid of the royal chateaux of the Paris region, with its uncouth layout and its lack of a clear style, is the only one to have kept its traditional role. The park, with its fine pools, and above all the forest, justify the choice and give the edifice a most splendid setting.

The chateau of Choisy became royal property in 1739: the structure had been completed only a half-century earlier. In 1680 the Grande Mademoiselle, who knew Choisy well, as she had fought there during the Fronde, had bought in that village above the Seine a piece of ground belonging to President Gonthier. She took Le Nôtre there, but he was not the least enthusiastic about the estate. 'You only see the river through a loophole!' he said to the King. Mlle de Montpensier was offended and asked Jacques Gabriel to erect a large single-storeyed building with Mansart-like stables and a balustrade. A pediment in the centre broke the monotony of these gables that were lighted by small dormer windows. At each end a pavilion protruded slightly from the main building. Gabriel asked Le Hongre, Le Moyne, Blanchard and Van der Meulen to carry out the decorations. Finally, Le Nôtre laid out a smallish parterre in front of the edifice, with an octagonal basin at the end. A large terrace spread in front of the façade overlooking the Seine, which could be seen 'from every side of the house and from the end of every alley', which pleased the owner very much. A drawing by Mariette has preserved for us an impression of the bowling green and of the green arbours Le Nôtre was obliged to preserve to satisfy Mme de Montpensier's rustic tastes. A belvedere with a ceiling painted by Coypel gave an even better view over the panorama that stretched from the triumphal arch at the Barrière du Trone to the forest of Sénart.

Before she died, Mme de Montpensier bequeathed Choisy to the Dauphin, who took possession on April 12, 1693. There he entertained actresses, but restricted his building to a few additions to the outhouses by Hardouin-Mansart. Louis XIV thought the place too far from Versailles. As early as 1696 he induced his son to exchange it for Meudon, which was too big for Louvois's widow. She did not lose by the exchange: she was given Choisy as well as 400,000 livres. She lived there until 1716. Then the chateau belonged to the Princesse de Conti, who added a gallery. Afterwards it passed to the Duc de la Valliere, her nephew. He sold it to Louis XV, and the estate was henceforth known as Choisy-le-Roi.

The Well-Beloved became attached to the house. For thirty years Ange-Jacques Gabriel, the original builder's grandson, altered it by adding wings, outbuildings, an orangery, aviaries, and so on. Panels by Verbeckt, piers by Chardin, paintings by Boucher and Gobelin tapestries decorated the interior. For his own pleasure the King had a pavilion built between 1754 and 1756: the Petit

Chateau, of which, in 1952, Georges Poisson revealed a delightful façade, decorated with garlands sculpted by Coustou. Oudry, Desportes and Verbeckt all contributed to the decoration of a house in which Louis XV passed many happy days with the Marquise de Pompadour. She was happy at Choisy: close by was the forest of Sénart, where she had first fallen in love with the King. . . .

As for the gardens, Gabriel had them enlarged and altered: English lawns with flowering borders, lime tree bowers, surrounded by iron arches and enlivened by tulips and hyacinths. There were masses of flowers to dazzle the eyes: lilac, roses and judas trees. The geometrician Dubois laid out the thickets which stretched down to the Seine. Statues embellished the park: the *Abondance* was a portrait of the Marquise (it was later taken to Menars). Coustou made a Mercury for the Bosquet de la Paix, and Bouchardon sculpted *Love cutting his bow from Hercules' club*, which is now in the Louvre.

Louis XV came often to Choisy with the Marquise. Comedies were acted there and ballets presented. After the death of Mme de Pompadour, the Comtesse du Barry came to Choisy in her turn. But by that time Louis XV was no longer interested in the chateau. For him its walls were too deeply impregnated with the remembrance of his great-grandfather's mistresses. Moreover, a climate of austerity prevailed at court and the King was thinking of demolishing some of the chateaux amongst his estates.

Choisy was spared and was even properly looked after until 1788. In that year the King ordered the furniture to be removed and the chateau turned into barracks for the Swiss Guards, but the plan was frustrated by the Revolution. The chateau was not destroyed by the revolutionaries, but abandoned, looted and demolished little by little. The town hall was built in the park, the rest was sold. Yet a few fragments are left: the entrance pavilions, a façade of the Petit Château, and a small part of the Grand Commune. All this is obscured in the midst of modern houses and is slowly disintegrating. Choisy is no more than a name, and only a few old prints help us to picture for ourselves the former beauty and luxury of this royal residence.

It is the same with Bellevue. Among clusters of modern houses, it is difficult to piece together the last remains of the chateau Mme de Pompadour built at Meudon to receive her royal lover. The site was wonderfully chosen. At the top of the Meudon hill, above the curves of the Seine, the view spreads over a huge prospect extending as far as Mont Valérien, over the Bois de Boulogne and the whole of Paris.

It was in 1748 that the Marquise began to purchase pieces of land destined to become parts of her estate, and for ten years her agent Colin was completing, with the Meudon notary, deeds whose purpose was to enlarge her park. But the chateau, which was at first a simple country house, was finished as early as 1750. It was built by Lassurance, Mme de Pompadour's usual architect. It is possible, but not certain, that Ange-Jacques Gabriel provided the plans. The chateau stood on the edge of the terrace and overlooked the valley. There was a main building between two wings, which included the guard-room, the baths and outhouses. The King opened the house on November 25, 1750, when the work was scarcely complete. The fireplaces smoked and it was icy cold. Everybody was delighted, or said so.

Bellevue's great luxury was its gardens. Flower beds ran along the terrace, but alleys, crossing and recrossing one another, ran down a quite steep slope towards Brimborion. The park spread to the south, facing the chateau's other façade. A big avenue climbed an easy slope towards the Sèvres warren and ended at an oval basin. At the top of the Tapis Vert stood Pigalle's statue of Louis XV in Genoan marble. The Tapis Vert divided the gardens in two: a maze, bowers and clusters of trees were thickly spread in pleasant compositions, decorated naturally with statues and basins. A statue of Friendship, also by Pigalle, had the features of Mme de Pompadour. It is said that it was put there to replace a statue of Love when the King ceased intimate relations with his one-time mistress. The Waterfall bower was among the best decorated; its panels of white marble, its trophies and its statues aroused widespread admiration.

To decorate the interior of the chateau, the Marquise de Pompadour summoned the artists she always patronised: Boucher, Oudry and Caffieri shared the work. A theatre, which replaced the one in the Little Apartments at Versailles, was decorated in Chinese style, which was the fashion of the time. A few plays were acted there. The Marquise continued to improve her estate: the main avenue was extended to the chateau's main gate, and she had two ice-houses built, but these were the last. At the beginning of the war against England and Prussia she decided to restrict her way of living. Bellevue cost her, for wages alone, 11,000 livres a year; so that, feeling very sad, she decided to get rid of it. But she did not lose it completely. In 1757 she made it over to Louis XV.

He came there several times. When the Marquise died, he took her successor, Mme du Barry, there. But Bellevue was too small for him, so he decided to join the side buildings by two little wings. In 1773, a few months before his death, these two wings were replaced by larger ones. He made Bellevue really comfortable: a new luxury was central heating by hot water that circulated through pipes under the floor.

In the reign of Louis XV, Bellevue was the scene of two epoch-making events: the secret discussions that led to an alliance between the Empress Maria-Theresa and the Most Christian King took place there between the Austrian Ambassador Kaunitz and the King's representative, Bernis. Actually, they took place both at Bellevue and Brimborion. The Marquise de Pompadour was often present. As for the treaty itself, it was signed by the French Secretary of State for Foreign Affairs, Rouillé, in his own chateau at Jouy-en-Josas. Another important decree was signed at Bellevue: the one by which high military rank was no longer reserved for noblemen alone.

After the King's death, Bellevue went to his three surviving daughters – Louis XVI's aunts, Adelaide, Victoire and Sophie. 'Mesdames' were surrounded by a little court and many servants. They changed the interior of the chateau very little. On the other hand, they enlarged the estate on the Meudon side as far as the Route des Gardes, and entrusted Lesage and Mique with the task of laying out an English garden with all the usual trappings on this new terrain: a river, a lake, winding lanes and little structures – a few cottages, a farm and a tower standing on some rocks, known as 'Marlborough's tower' after the old song which had just become popular again (*Malbrouk s'en va-t-en guerre*).

In 1791 the two surviving princesses, Adelaide and Victoire, decided to leave France. Rumour of their going began to spread and they had to leave precipitately. They were allowed to disappear, and in Rome they ended an existence that was without glory. When they had left, Bellevue, looted and defaced, was requisitioned. Volunteers were housed there, who showed no respect for the panels and tapestries. In 1796 the department of Seine-et-Oise acquired the estate and sold it the next year to a certan Têtu, who pulled down some of the outbuildings. The breaking-up process began and continued until 1823, when the whole chateau, apart from its north wing, was completely demolished. Southwards the estate was preserved until 1878. Today a few fragments of the wings remain, hidden among modern houses. From the terrace, reached over two sloping alleys, one may look out upon a landscape Mme de Pompadour would no longer recognize. To use the words of Georges Poisson, this 'mounting tide of new houses, dominated by the massive Renault factory has deprived it of all its charm.

As for the Brimborion pavilion, at the foot of the hill which descends towards the Seine, it had sheltered the love affair of the King and Madame de Pompadour. Later it became the house of the governor of the estate, and was pulled down in 1878. The land surrounding it was sold, but the view had already been much altered by the building of the railway.

It may be questioned whether Louveciennes (commonly called Luciennes) has a right to be included among the royal chateaux. Its name is indissolubly associated with the Comtesse du Barry and consequently with Louis XV. Yet one forgets that in fact the estate had been part of the Royal properties for more than a century. In 1700 Louis XIV had a house built at the top of the hill above the Seine and the Marly Waterworks which was intended to house the engineers who operated them. It comprised a main building with a square pavilion at either side. During the eighteenth century the house changed hands several times, passing from Mlle de la Tourbe d'Estrées to Mlle de Clermont, but the King still owned it, and in 1741 he gave it to the Comtesse de Toulouse. Thus

91

Louveciennes descended to her son, the Duc de Penthièvre. He did not need it, being amply supplied with chateaux already. He gave it back to the King. That is how Louis XV was able to present it to his mistress Jeanne Bécu, Comtesse du Barry.

She was delighted with the gift. Louveciennes became a haven of peace, the permanent dream of all the leading characters in the harassing life of the court. She had the drawing-room and dining-room decorated with panelling. The vestibule was given a frieze, but she concentrated above all on the gardens.

As early as 1770, she made Ledoux build at the edge of the hill, above the valley, a pavilion in neo-Greek style which was then in high fashion. The plan was very simple. The central structure was preceded by a peristyle which projected only slightly and consisted of four pillars. Behind was an oval dining-room, which was succeeded by a drawing-room with a boudoir and a card-room at either side. Lecomte decorated the interior of the peristyle with a frieze in bas-relief representing children playing with a ram in the midst of roses. All the bronze ornaments were sculpted by Gouthière. The greatest skill was used to make a perfect jewel of Ledoux' pavilion. In front of it was an 'English' garden and a charming lawn bordered with flowers. A Temple of Love – its absence would have been surprising – was also built by Ledoux in another part of the park.

Louis XV liked Louveciennes. Moreau le Jeune has given us a picture of the King and his mistress having supper with a few friends in the vestibule-dining-room, under the eye of Zemor, the negro who later betrayed his employer. A clever piece of machinery raised an already prepared table from the basement. Returning to Marly from a hunt, a halt at Louveciennes was for the King the pleasantest of diversions.

After his death, the favourite was invited to take refuge in the Abbey of Pont-aux-Dames. Yet Louis XVI eventually gave Louveciennes back to her. She spent some happy days there with her new protector, the Duc de Brissac, but he was slaughtered at Versailles in September 1792 and the murderers cast his head at the poor woman's feet. An international gang of swindlers stole her jewels, and the Comtesse was obliged to go several times to London, where the men had been caught. That was enough to have her charged as an 'emigre'. She was arrested, sentenced to death by the Revolutionary Tribunal and executed, having never understood a thing of what was happening to her.

Her chateau had already been looted. The estate was sold many times between 1795 and the present day. Among its transitory owners was Ouvrard, banker and Army Commissary, who was finally arrested by Napoleon I, though that was not the end of his surprising career. In 1830 another banker, Lafitte, was the owner of Louveciennes; he restored the gardens. Dr Blancheton, the author of the *Vues pittoresques des châteaux de la France*, wrote that year: 'The park is better laid out today than in the days of its fame . . . M. Lafitte has added fountains, pools and small structures with delightful effect.' That may be, but the banker may be reproached for having sold half the estate. In fact, he sold Mme du Barry's pavilion about 1840, so that henceforth that chateau and the pavilion led different lives. The latter belonged to Loucheur, a minister who restored the interior extensively. Between the two World Wars it was owned by the scent-maker Coty, who had the pavilion removed and rebuilt, stone by stone, which was more or less justifiable by reason of the condition it was in. But it is a pity that a superfluous upper storey was added.

The park is still very fine. Here and there are a few reminders of the favourite: the acacia at the foot of which it is said she hid her jewels; the King's Alley, the Temple of Love, and also the delightful view of the valley still to be enjoyed from the top of the hill.

The Bagatelle pavilion in the Bois de Boulogne had its origin in a bet between the Comte d'Artois and Marie-Antoinette. But before it was built, in a matter of weeks, there had been an estate on the same site, the history of which is worth telling.

First of all, at the beginning of the eighteenth century, there was a little menagerie there, on the site of which an advocate-general built a house, which was bought by the Marshal d'Estrées, who replaced it with a charming pavilion which he named Babiole.

A parliamentary councillor, the Marquis de Boisgelin and the Prince de Chimay lived there one after the other. Finally, in 1775, the Comte d'Artois bought the estate for 36,000 livres. That was when he bet Marie-Antoinette that he would build a pavilion there in less than three months. The architect Bellanger was given the job, and within sixty-four days, between September 23 and November 26, 1777, Bagatelle was built. Artois won his bet of 100,000 livres, but the pavilion had cost him more than three million.

It was a tour-de-force, nevertheless, and the name of the place is a reminder of the bet: *bagatella* in Italian means a bauble, a trifling thing. The entrance and the Pavillon des Pages have disappeared, but the main pavilion has kept its original design, with a cupola and a protruding salon on the other side. It is a pity that nineteenth century alterations deprived the exterior of some of its charm and discreet refinement. In 1860 the roof was raised and the dome was hidden by a balustrade, while a balcony replaced the archway above the entrance.

As luck would have it, and despite the restorations, the interior has retained all its beauty: it is still possible to admire the Pompeian style which was so fashionable at the end of the eighteenth century: the billiards room and its friezes, and its carved panelling by Lhuillier, the big salon with panels depicting the rivalry of Love and War, and the music room, all uniting the exquisite fancies of a prince with beauty and richness.

As for the gardens, a triumph of the 'English' style, they were among the most famous in France. Planted by the Scottish gardener Blaikie, they were made rather slowly from 1777 onwards. There were many small buildings, brooks, bridges and winding glades. In front of the pavilion was a bowling green enclosed by bowers, and the river ran out of a lake at the foot of a precipitous rock. It flowed beside the Philosopher's House of multi-coloured windows to remind one of the diversity of human passions which colour the same object with different tones. There was a Lover's Bridge and a Chinese Bridge, and a Palladio Bridge, which did not last long because it was made of wood. One came finally to an island with the tomb of the King of Hearts and to the antique tomb. Everywhere were statues, vases and seats of grass. There was no ordered plan in an ensemble that was meant to please the eye, according to Dulaure, with a picture of rustic nature, like the informal dress of a coquette. During the Revolution Bagatelle was turned into a sort of funfair. Napoleon bought back the estate for 300,000 livres. The Duc de Berry became its owner during the Restoration and the Children of France played there. Louis-Philippe sold it in 1835 to Lord Seymour, the Marquis of Hertford, who altered the pavilion unsuccessfully. The gardens had already suffered some changes and a Gothic craze caused the substitution of a belvedere for the Paladin's Tower and the ruins of an abbey . . . Lord Seymour's son, Richard Wallace, housed his collection in his own 'Trianon'. His secretary sold Bagatelle to the town of Paris in 1905 for six million francs. In the park the celebrated rose garden was then created, which attracts several thousands of visitors every year, more perhaps than the pavilion of the Comte d'Artois.

CHAPTER V

IMPERIAL PALACES

THE names of some chateaux are indissolubly associated with the princes who made them the framework of their own lives. Charles V and Vincennes; Francis I and Fontainebleau; Louis XIV and Versailles. Compiègne cannot be dissociated from memories of the Empress Eugénie, nor Malmaison from Josephine's graceful shade. But while Malmaison, before it was bought by General Bonaparte's wife, was only an obscure house, without history, yet Compiègne's past was long and glorious. Other castles can conjure up Imperial splendour, but Compiègne is deeply impregnated with it.

In its present external aspect Compiègne seems to the visitor rather heavy and monotonous. It dates from the middle eighteenth century, but the estate itself belonged to the kings of France for more than twelve centuries before that. Gregory of Tours states, in fact, that the Merovingian sovereigns had an estate there in the sixth century. Childebert I signed a diploma there in 557. Clotaire, Clovis' grandson, died there in 561, and the wagons of the so-called 'indolent kings' often stopped before the royal palace of Compiègne, which was undoubtedly a modest one. It probably stood near Notre-Dame, which later became the Abbey of Saint Corneille. This monastery was founded by Charles the Bald, who is also credited with the reconstruction of the castle. One thing is certain, that the Carolingian princes – the last of them, mostly – stayed gladly at Compiègne, and the Capetians who succeeded them remained faithful to the tradition. Louis II, 'the Stammerer', Louis V, and Hugues, Hugues Capet's grandson, are buried in Saint Corneille, and the town grew up round their residence.

Yet it seems that the Carolingian castle was abandoned later for some other building. The town was now surrounded with ramparts. A strong keep, central redoubt and royal dwelling was built near the banks of the Oise before the reign of St Louis. The big tower called Beauregard is all that survives.

Finally, in the fourteenth century, a new castle was built at the edge of the town, closer to the forest. It is mentioned in 1380. This castle stood on the site of the present building but was much smaller. It was erected by Charles V and was one of the elements of the defence of the town, the ramparts of which had been strengthened by the King. It was at the foot of those high walls that Joan of Arc was captured in 1430. Was she imprisoned, after her capture, in the great tower that still survives? It is not unlikely.

After it had been occupied by the Anglo-Burgundians, Charles V's old fortress passed through the centuries with few changes. Most kings stayed at Compiègne, but only briefly, on the eve of a day's hunting, and not one of them thought of transforming the castle which, at the time of Louis XIV, still largely preserved its fourteenth century structure. Yet Marie de Medici, rebelling against her son's orders, was sent there in disgrace after the Day of Dupes. She managed to escape and reached Flanders just as, a few years earlier, she had escaped from the chateau of Blois through a window, by sliding down a rope. A strange activity for a dowager!

Anne of Austria, Mazarin and Louis XIV took refuge there during the Fronde. The young King's recollections of the place were not pleasant: 'I am housed in Compiègne like a peasant,' he once said, laughing. Yet he returned there to hunt quite often. Intent on giving his grandson, the Duke of Burgundy, a perfect military education, he had his troops manoeuvre in the neighbourhood in 1698. Naturally, the camp at Compiègne must have been the scene of some splendid festivities.

Meanwhile, the old castle resisted the assaults of time. Louis XIV was too interested in Versailles to hand it over to the architects. On the other hand, his great-grandson decided to transform Compiègne into a truly royal residence. This tireless traveller tried to defeat his boredom by changing his surroundings, as if he found the mistresses who accompanied him more attractive when seen in a new setting. Work began in 1738. Jacques Gabriel was in charge. When he died in 1742, his son Ange-Jacques carried on.

It was a difficult task. The King's intention was to live at Compiègne when he wanted to, works or no works. This involved pulling down and rebuilding without upsetting the court. That is why Jacques Gabriel and his son kept the triangular plan formerly justified by the outline of the ramparts, but was no longer justifiable in the eighteenth century. They used the old foundations and even kept a few walls. Actually, they greatly lengthened the palace. Moreover, the sloping terrace enabled them to have the first floor in the main courtyard on the same level as the ground floor of the huge façade that stretched slantwise along the garden terrace.

Work went on for forty years. It caused an endless 'general post' among the apartments, so that the King lived in 1740 in what later became the ushers' room and the Emperor's apartments. Shortage of money did not allow Gabriel to carry out the original plan which would have made the castle as big as Versailles. When the architect left in 1775, Compiègne was far from being finished. Le Dreux de la Châtre, his pupil, built the colonnade, completed the façade and the

staircases and supervized the interior decoration of Marie-Antoinette's apartments. All was finished by 1786.

It was confiscated by the Revolutionary government and its demolition was suggested. But this was a mere threat. The gardens suffered more. In 1800 the Consulate installed at Compiègne a school for future officers. It was transferred to Châlons-sur-Marne in 1806, when the Emperor decided to restore the chateau to its original purpose. Percier and Fontaine were entrusted with the arrangements. Louis XVI's and Marie-Antoinette's apartments were transformed and decorated in the neo-antique style which was then in fashion. Charles IV of Spain, who had lost his Spanish throne, his wife and her lover, Godoy, were housed there.

After the repudiation, Napoleon, intent on acquiring ancestors (and heirs) went to meet the new Empress of the French at Compiègne. The scene, which took place on March 28, 1810, has often been described. The Emperor hurried the court presentations of the kings, queens, princesses and marshals who were massed along the staircases and the great state salons. He was in a hurry to be alone with his young wife. After a private and very gay dinner for three – the Emperor, the Empress and Caroline Murat[1] – Napoleon hastened to join his wife, Uncle Fesch having obligingly affirmed that their marriage by proxy was valid. Napoleon's remark, the next day, to his aide-de-camp is well known: 'Marry a German, my dear fellow; they are the best wives in the world, sweet, kind, naive and as fresh as roses.'

During the last years of the Empire, Napoleon and Marie-Louise often came to Compiègne. Marie-Louise loved the place, just as the Empress Eugénie loved it half a century later.

In 1814, what was left of the Grande Armée fought its last battle at Compiègne. In the Salon du Grand Couvert, the Emperor's former *salle-à-manger*, Louis XVIII met the Czar Alexander in a momentous interview. But Louis XVIII and his brother, Charles X, seldom came again. Louis-Philippe did not like those big and solemn halls, the pompous decorations of which did not appeal to his bourgeois taste. Yet during his reign the chapel witnessed an historical event: on August 9, 1832, the King of the Belgians, Leopold, married Princess Louise, the French King's daughter.

But Compiègne was to experience a greater glory under the Second Empire. It is difficult to see why Napoleon III, and especially the Empress, became so obsessed with a palace of such cold and austere architecture, so very different from the fashion of the time. It may be that recollections of the King's uncle haunted his spirit. Or that Compiègne was perfect to house a large number of guests. For fifteen years the Compiègne 'round' was much sought after by Paris society. Yet the interior decoration had changed but little: the furniture had

[1] Napoleon's sister.

been changed for the style of the Second Empire. The most brilliant festivities and the most sumptuous receptions followed one upon the other. In the former Salon des Cartes, the guests used to assemble. They played at little drawing-room games or danced to the sound of a shrill mechanical piano with Morny turning the handle. Comedies were improvised in the Emperor's former dining-room, with Viollet-le-Duc acting as prompter. Card games were played in Napoleon's former Council Chamber, and the ministers met in the Emperor's former library. For those who want to know about court life during the Second Empire and the style of that light-headed but restless period, Compiègne offers a unique ensemble. The museum which has been established in the former guests' apartments enables one to rediscover the setting and the characters, from Winterhalter's well-known painting to the touching relics of the Prince Imperial.

The last French court went down to the music of Offenbach. The Prussians occupied Compiègne. Thirty years later the Czar and his Empress stayed there, and their stay symbolized the rebirth of France and its return to the body of the leading European nations. A hundred years after the Grande Armée's disaster, the German onrush stopped at Compiègne. Since 1917 the French G.H.Q. had been established there and remained there until April 1918. And it was in the forest of Compiègne that on November 11, 1918, the Armistice was signed. The chateau was damaged by bombardment at the end of the First World War, but was restored immediately.

Its external aspect is cold and heavy. The long colonnade which connects the two pavilions at the entrance to the main courtyard, and the main building at the back with its two wings, are better suited to a town palace (the Palais-Royal, more or less its contemporary) than to a country chateau. Yet the immense façade which forms the side of the triangle that faces the park is harmonious, and its sober grandeur modifies the monotonous character of the structure.

Within, Marie-Antoinette's apartments have recovered the furniture which was there during her reign. At Compiègne, as at Versailles, an effort is being made to instal authentic furniture in the setting for which it had been intended. Great patience is called for, since successive sales and the various encroachments of the Mobilier National make such a reconstruction very difficult. Success is slow, but at Compiègne these efforts have had some happy results.

Thus the rooms of the Emperor and Marie-Louise contain the furniture made for them by Jacob. Elsewhere, Second Empire furniture, often selected by the Empress herself, has replaced the furniture that Napoleon knew. But the decoration of the walls has been respected. Redouté and Dubois were the principal originators. Girofet painted a few ceilings. The Gobelin tapestries, the Lyon silks and the seats in the salon have kept their opulence and their freshness.

Thus Compiègne has one of the richest museums of the two Empires. Moreover, in what was the kitchen courtyard a number of coaches and carriages have been collected. There is the ceremonial Elysée berlin and the caterpillar truck used for the Croisière Noire,[1] the Grand Bi of 1900 and the very first motor-cars. The museum is terribly overcrowded and will soon have to find other quarters.

Despite many alterations at the beginning of the nineteenth century, the park has retained its elegance. It stretches along the large transverse façade. Gabriel had to face a delicate problem: the terrain was flat and without water-courses. He remained faithful to Le Nôtre's traditions. He set up several levels on successive terraces, the first of which bordered the chateau. The second was decorated with flower beds. The third framed an 'English' plot of two long sections ending in a bowling green. Yew trees flanked this plot and masked the green arbours. The Tapis Vert closed the design where the King's Alley entered the forest.

Berthault altered the park on Napoleon's orders. The supports of the terraces bordering the façades were replaced by a gently sloping bank giving access to coaches through a central avenue. Lawns replaced the flower beds, and irregular clumps replaced the geometrical designs of the 'French' garden.

After Napoleon's marriage to Marie-Louise, an ironwork arbour some kilo-metres long was erected on the left of the garden. Climbing plants were made to cover it to remind the Empress of some aspects of Schönbrunn. Statues filled the park and a magnificent road across the forest, the Avenue des Beauxmonts, lengthened the vista by four kilometres. The park had kept the appearance that Napoleon gave it.

If Marie-Louise and Eugénie de Montijo still reign over the palace of Compiègne, it is the light and charming shade of Josephine de Beauharnais who awaits the visitor to the chateau at Malmaison. Hardly a chateau, but rather a large and comfortable country house, fit for magistrates or rich bankers.

It did not appear in history before the beginning of the seventeenth century. This rather sinister name is not associated with any particular tragedy. Was it a house of evil repute? We are not certain. It is likely that the monks of St Denis, who owned the place in the Middle Ages, had built a leper house there. Afterwards there was a farm there and wealthy farmers, whose names are often found in the parish registers of Rueil, the neighbouring village.

In 1662 the estate was acquired by a Parliamentary Councillor of Paris, Christophe Perrot. Perrot had a quite simple building erected: a central block, flanked by higher pavilions protruding from the façade. The slate roofs were pierced by two dormer-windows. It was a large house, with two lines of windows, those of the second floor, below the roof, being shorter than those of the first, which were also shorter than the big windows of the ground floor. Such, at least, is the present aspect, which has doubtless suffered a few changes since Perrot's time.

The Perrot family owned Malmaison until the middle of the eighteenth cen-

[1] The north-south crossing of Africa.

tury. Then it passed to the Barentin family, who did not live there but rented it to financiers, rich enough to embellish it. They were M de la Jonchère, M de Boulogne, and M Desfourniel, who entertained writers there and philosophers connected with Mme Harenc and Marmontel. In 1771 the family of Coulteux du Molay bought it and the chateau became the centre of a little group of artists and writers. Mme Vigée-Lebron[1] and the Abbé Sièyes[2] used to go there, and Delille.[3]

On April 21, 1799, for the sum of 325,000 francs, Josephine Tascher de la Pagerie, the wife of General Bonaparte, became the proprietor of the Malmaison estate, sold to her by M Le Coulteux du Molay. That is how the peaceful house of Christophe Perrot entered history. Josephine knew the region well. She had lived at Croissy, on the right bank of the Seine, then at St Cloud, from where had begun, a few months later, the incredible destiny of the lean little general she had married. After the 18th Brumaire, the Tuileries became the First Consul's palace, but Josephine did not abandon Malmaison. All through the Consulate the chateau was Bonaparte's place of rest. He sometimes went there for longer periods, to hold councils or to receive some illustrious person. But it was mostly for rest that he went there, to forget the worries and burdens of office. He relaxed there and, according to Bourienne, became pleasant and human, playing like a child. He delighted to see Josephine walking along the paths.

She had fallen in love with the estate. She extended the park up to the St Cucufa ponds. She decorated the chateau with fabrics. With perfect taste she transformed the gardens with a 'Consular Trianon', where the loveliest women of the time and the most brilliant officers came together to form a glittering court. Writers used to come, too: Ducis, Bernardin de St Pierre, Marie-Joseph Chénier, artists like Talma, painters like Girodet or Gérard. Plays and ballets were performed, and games were organized.

After her marriage had been annulled in 1809 it was naturally to Malmaison that the ex-Empress made her discreet retirement. She died there on May 29, 1814, during the Emperor's exile on Elba. He too returned to Malmaison. After Waterloo he took refuge there, wondering what the future would be. He spent four days there, June 25th to 29th, conjuring up the radiant memory of the one who had accompanied him on his prodigious ascent to power. His fate was sealed. From Malmaison he left for Rochefort, the first stage on the road to St Helena.

Eugéne de Beauharnais inherited the estate and took part of the furniture to Bavaria, where he had married. When he died the chateau was sold to a Swedish banker and the park was broken up. After belonging for a while to Queen Maria-

[1] French eighteenth century portrait painter (1768-1820).
[2] A member of the French assemblies during the Revolution and one of the three Consuls (1748-1836).
[3] French poet and translator (1783-1813).

Christina of Spain, Malmaison was bought by Napoleon III and the Empress Eugénie piously brought together some souvenirs of the Consulate and the Empire.

There was fighting in the park during the war of 1870. Then the estate was sold again in 1877 and further dividing-up reduced its extent. The house was finally bought by a banker, Daniel Osiris, who generously gave it back to the nation in 1904. Two years later the museum was opened. Thanks to the curators' efforts, it is a large one. Magnificent gifts have enriched it. A short time ago the chateau of Boispreau was added to Malmaison: it was the gift of an American benefactor, Edward Tuck. Thus the museum has been completed with furniture and relics of the King of Rome.

According to Jean Bourbguinon, its devoted curator for many years, Malmaison is now a museum of art, and a museum of history, but above all a museum of remembrance. One may not like the Empire style, or the cold and pompous furniture Jacob made for most rooms, but one cannot escape being moved when entering the Empress' room. This famous room, in the shape of a tent, has been carefully reconstructed even to the carved and gilded bed in which Josephine died.

Gold-embroidered curtains have doubtless replaced the original hangings of crimson cashmere. But the secretaire, the bronze pedestal table, and the writing table are still there, and so is the harp in the dining-room, which seems to be awaiting the Empress' slender fingers.

> *Malmaison n'est qu'un soupir.*
> *Tout s'y courbe, tout s'y dérobe*
> *A la douce façon créole.*
> *C'est un lieu de grande langueur*
> *Urne pour la cendre d'un coeur....*[1]

Those moving lines by the Comtesse de Noailles return to one's thoughts as one walks along the lanes of the park, where in the Spring the fragrance of the Empress' roses may still be breathed.

The gardens of Malmaison cast an endless spell. Josephine was not alone responsible for their creation. M Le Coulteux du Molay had asked the architect Morel to plan an 'English' garden, the very one that had been admired and praised in verse by the Abbé Delille. But after the estate had been bought and enlarged, Berthault had been made to contrive some new gardens. In front of the castle, the lawn is transversed by streams which emerge from a small temple of four red-marble columns. They merge into a pool that winds across the grass and then into the park. Statues sent by Alexandre Le Noir, the founder of the

---

[1] Malmaison is only a sigh. Everything yields there to the gentle creole manner. It is a place of great languor, an urn for the ashes of a heart. . . .

Musée des Monuments Français, decorate the alleys. There was also a grotto, a funerary bas-relief – and the 'tomb' that was traditional to all 'English' gardens – and even two rostral columns that came from Richelieu's castle at Rueil.

The furthest part of the park has been less elegantly designed. One passes insensibly from subjugate nature to nature still wild. Yet near the pond and wood of St Cucufa, the Swiss hamlet with its sheep-fold and its cowshed is in the best Trianon tradition.

Very little is left of a park which once covered many hundreds of acres. Luckily, the finest part has been preserved, especially the gardens which, on Isabey's advice, Josephine decorated with more than 250 different kinds of roses (she had a great love of roses) together with geraniums, dahlias, hydrangeas, hibiscus and rhododendrons.

In 1800 she planted the cedar tree which commemorated the victory of Marengo. It still spreads its branches wide, and Joséphine's rose garden is still splendid in the spring. The palaces of kings and emperors may now be mere sanctuaries of remembrance, but the parks that surround them, when they are properly looked after, keep all their exuberance and live their own lives when those who created them have long turned to dust. Such is the revenge, one may say, of nature over man.

ILLUSTRATIONS

The following explanatory list relates to the illustrations to be found
all together at the end of the book, except for the colour plates which
are placed as indicated below.

COLOUR PLATES

BLACK AND WHITE PLATES

15. GISORS. The keep. The castle was begun in the eleventh century and is today a ruin. It was the scene of numerous attacks by Philippe-Auguste and Richard Coeur-de-Lion in turns.

16. DOURDAN. Towers and moats. About 1220, Philippe-Auguste built the feudal wall flanked by eight topless towers. The keep rose ninety feet above the moat.

17. PIERREFONDS. General view of the castle. Built by Louis of Orleans, the fortress was pulled down in the seventeenth century. Viollet-le-Duc's restoration allows us to see its importance in the history of military architecture.

18. PIERREFONDS. Statue of Viollet-le-Duc as St James Major at the chapel door.

19. FONTAINEBLEAU. The Francis I Gallery. Detail of woodwork. The salamander was the King's emblem.

20. FONTAINEBLEAU. General view of the façade overlooking the water.

21 to 23. FONTAINEBLEAU. Details of the King's staircase. Sculptures by Primaticcio decorating Anne de Pisseleu's famous room.

24. FONTAINEBLEAU. The ballroom, known as the Henry II Gallery. The ceiling of this huge hall is the work of Philibert Delorme who entrusted Primaticcio with the decoration.

25. FONTAINEBLEAU. The Council Chamber. Built under Francis I, it was decorated by Boucher, van Loo and J. B. Pierre in 1753.

26. FONTAINEBLEAU. Marie-Antoinette's room. The boudoir. The Rousseau brothers decorated this room which was finished by Mique. The chimney bronzes are by Gouthière.

27. FONTAINEBLEAU. The throne room. Former royal bedchamber. The carved ceiling is from the period of Louis XIII. The throne was made by Jacob in 1905.

28. FONTAINEBLEAU. Aerial view.

29. FONTAINEBLEAU. The Francis I Wing. Also known as the Minister's Wing. It was part of the group of buildings erected by Gilles le Breton about 1528.

30. FONTAINEBLEAU. The Louis XV Wing. Built by Gabriel in 1738. It replaced one of the Renaissance wings.

31. FONTAINEBLEAU. The castle seen from the park.

32. FONTAINEBLEAU. The pavilion and the carp pool. Rebuilt on Napoleon's orders, it was restored in the nineteenth century.

33. MEUDON. The terrace seen from the Observatory. It was built by Abel Servien, Marquis de Sablé, in the seventeenth century.

34. MEUDON. Statue in the park.

35. MEUDON. The chateau, after a contemporary engraving.

36. MEUDON. The Orangery. It dates from the days of the Princess of Lorraine who lived in the 'old chateau', which was demolished in 1804.

37. VILLERS-COTTERETS. The façade overlooking the park. Built by Francis I about 1520, the castle's principal architects were J. and G. Le Breton.

38. VILLERS-COTTERETS. The loggia of the Logis du Roi.

39. VILLERS-COTTERETS. The staircase ceiling of the State Room.

40. VILLERS-COTTERETS. Detail from the façade of the Logis du Roi. The salamander of Francis I. This emblem appears on most of the buildings raised at the King's orders.

41. VILLERS-COTTERETS. The State Room. Reredos of 1539. The room was turned into a chapel about the end of the sixteenth century.

42. VILLERS-COTTERETS. Detail from a ceiling of the second staircase of the State Room. Venus and Satyr.

43. VILLERS-COTTERETS. Chimney with the arms of Francis I.

44. SAINT-GERMAIN. The inner courtyard. Its harmonious architecture allows the light to play upon the elegant buttresses and red brickwork.

45. SAINT-GERMAIN. General view. Built by Pierre Chambige in the reign of Francis I, it was recklessly restored in the nineteenth century.

46. SAINT-GERMAIN. Courtyard from above.

47. SAINT-GERMAIN. The terrace. Overlooking the Seine and more than a mile and a half in length, it was built by Le Nôtre between 1669 and 1673.

48. SAINT-GERMAIN. The Château-Neuf after a contemporary engraving. It was destroyed at the end of the eighteenth century.

49. ANET. The castle after an old engraving.

50. ANET. The castle seen from the park. Built by Philibert Delorme as the residence of Diane de Poitiers. Only the west wing and the chapel survive. This wing was greatly changed in the seventeenth century by Louis de Vendôme.

51. ANET. Statue of Diane. The bronze original of Cellini's masterpiece is in the Louvre. It was carved by René Boyrin and it is said that the King's mistress was the model.

52 & 53. ANET. Vestibule and Grand Staircase. Louis de Vendôme, in the seventeenth century, commissioned Claude Desgots to construct this majestic staircase, the rails of which are ornamented with the Vendôme cipher.

54. ANET. The park. The canals, planned by Le Nôtre, are filled with water from the Eure. The trees are grouped in a less classical style.

55. ANET. The chapel. Altar and paving. The eliptical pattern of the paving produces some curious optical effects.

56. ANET. The chapel dome, where the design is on the same lines as in the paving.

57 & 58. ANET. The chapel. Sculptured angels in a bas-relief by the school of Jean Goujon.

59. SAINT-CLOUD. The Grand Cascade. The upper section, built for Monsieur by Lepautre, was restored by Mansart in 1697, when the lower basin was added.

60. VERSAILLES. The Ceres basin by Regnaudin, placed in 1672 at the intersection of the Summer walk and the Ceres walk.

61. VERSAILLES. The Bacchus basin, on the Autumn walk, was the work of the Marsy brothers and also dates from 1672.

62. VERSAILLES. The Hundred Steps. This staircase of rose-coloured marble connects the terrace above the Orangery with the Pièce d'eau des Suisses.

63 & 64. VERSAILLES. Façade overlooking the park. By adding his own creations to Le Vau's plan, Mansart gave these western façades their final aspect.

65. VERSAILLES. The Hall of Mirrors (Galerie des Glaces). Usually called the Grande Galerie. Built by Mansart between 1678 and 1687. The ceiling was decorated by Le Brun.

66 & 67. VERSAILLES. The theatre. Begun by Jacques-Ange Gabriel in 1757, it was only opened in 1779 on the occasion of the marriage of the Dauphin and Marie-Antoinette.

68. VERSAILLES. The Opera; detail of the woodwork.

69. VERSAILLES. The chapel. Built of white stone and placed at the centre of the north wing, it was planned by Mansart but completed in 1710 by his brother-in-law, Robert de Cotte.

70 to 73. VERSAILLES. Louis XV's rooms: tapestries, woodwork and furniture. These rooms, dating from 1738, have been skilfully restored in recent years.

74. VERSAILLES. Grand Trianon, built by Mansart in 1687, this Italian-style palace stands colourfully amid flower-filled parterres.

75. VERSAILLES. Petit Trianon. Interior of the French pavilion. Built by Gabriel in 1751 for Louis XV. The woodwork is by Verbeckt. The stucco frieze depicts farmyard animals.

76. VERSAILLES. The Queen's Hamlet. The farm. Originally comprising cowshed and stables, these buildings were recently restored. Mique designed these lighthearted structures for Marie-Antoinette.

77. VERSAILLES. Petit Trianon. The French Pavilion.

78. VERSAILLES. Petit Trianon. The octagonal Belvedere. The interior decorations were the work of Mique and conceived in the Pompeian style.

79. MARLY. The chateau after an old engraving. The way the twelve pavilions were placed to frame the central pavilion can be seen.

80. MARLY. 'Le Grand Miroir'.

81. SCEAUX. 'Le Grand Perspective'. The fountains have revived the atmosphere of the park in which so many brilliant festivities took place.

82. SCEAUX. The Pavilion of Aurora. Built by Claude Perrault and decorated by Le Brun, this elegant building was part of the Duc de Maine's estate.

83. CHANTILLY. General view from the park. In the centre, the Manche, the southern arm of the Grand Canal. On the extreme right, the Treasury Tower, which holds the rose Diamond.

84. CHANTILLY. Aerial view of the castle and terrace.

85. CHANTILLY. Horses on the tympanum of the Great Stables.

86. CHANTILLY. The Great Stables, built for the Duc de Bourbon, Louis XV's minister, by Jean Aubert.

87. CHANTILLY. The Canal; one of a series which surround the castle with water.

88. CHANTILLY. The Island of Love. This kiosk is situated in the new 'English' garden, was designed in 1820, and has under its roof a statue of Eros.

89 to 94. CHANTILLY. The Monkey Room; details and general view. The decorations are attributed to Christopher Huet.

95. CHANTILLY. Sylvie's house, built by Mansart on the site of the house given to the woman celebrated by Théophile Viau under the name of Sylvie: Marie-Félicité des Ursins, wife of the Maréchal de Montmorency.

96 to 99. CHANTILLY. Details of woodwork in Sylvie's house. Some of these seventeenth-century carvings came from a hunting lodge in the forest of Dreux.

100. CHANTILLY. Sylvie's pool.

101. CHANTILLY. The castle from the park. The main building, reconstructed in the nineteenth century, flanks the small chateau, or Capitainerie, built in the sixteenth century by Jean Bullant for the Constable de Montmorency.

102. CHOISY-LE-ROI. The chateau from a contemporary engraving. Nothing survives of this building.

103 & 104. CHOISY-LE-ROI. Two views of the park.

105 & 108. BRIMBORION. The park of Brimborion, between Bellevue and Sèvres. The very names evoke the charming country house to which Louis XV and the Marquise de Pompadour used to escape.

106. LOUVECIENNES. Louis XV gave this estate to Madame du Barry in 1769. The chateau had been built in Louis XIV's reign to house the engineer for the 'Marly Machine'.

107. CHOISY-LE-ROI. A pavilion.

109. RAMBOUILLET. Francis I's Tower. It was within these fourteenth-century walls that, according to tradition, the King died on March 31, 1547.

110. RAMBOUILLET. Corner turret on the façade overlooking the park and lake. Too heterogeneous to be harmonious, the castle looks out upon the par-

terre which was designed in the time of the Comte de Toulouse, and the fine sheets of water laid out by Fleuriau d'Armenonville.

111. RAMBOUILLET. Carving on the oak doors of the Assembly Rooms. This woodwork has been so scoured as to remove its gilded paintwork.

112. RAMBOUILLET. The Queen's Dairy. Built by Thévenin for Marie-Antoinette in 1785 and decorated by Pierre Julien; it stands beside the Farm, built for Louis XVI.

113. RAMBOUILLET. Delft tiling in the bathroom. This room is at the foot of the great tower and was decorated at the time of the Duc de Penthièvre.

114. BAGATELLE. The door of the Round Room.

115 & 116. BAGATELLE. Two views of the pavilion.

117. BAGATELLE. The dome of the Round Room.

118. COMPIEGNE. The carriage hall in the Musée de la Voiture.

119. COMPIEGNE. The Hall of Pillars. The busts and statues in the former royal entrance were put there by Napoleon.

120. COMPIEGNE. Façade overlooking the park. Louis XV gave Gabriel the task of building the present castle. Jacques-Ange, the architect's son, and afterwards Le Dreux de La Châtre, continued the work which was finished in 1784.

121. COMPIEGNE. The Emperor's bedroom. The furniture, with original furnishings has been placed in a décor planned by Percier and Fontaine.

122. COMPIEGNE. The ballroom. It was created for Napoleon I.

123. COMPIEGNE. The bedroom of the Empress Marie-Louise. The paintings of Aurora and the Four Seasons are by Girodet, and the furniture by Jacob.

124. MALMAISON. The music room. The bust of Josephine in the court of Chinard. The musical instruments were used by the Empress and Queen Hortense.

125. MALMAISON. The billiards room. The carpet was a gift to the Emperor from the King of Saxony in 1809.

126. MALMAISON. By skilful changes, Josephine made this seventeenth century house into the First Consul's favourite resort. The ex-Empress died here in 1814.

127 & 128. MALMAISON. The library. The Emperor's desk and the statue of Bonaparte during the Egyptian campaign by Marton. This room alone preserves its original décor.

129. MALMAISON. The Emperor's death mask.

The photographs illustrating this book are the property of Editions Arthaud and are by M. Henri Pallaison, except for the following: 3: Archives Photographiques. 24: Bertault (Ed. Arthaud). 28: photo Pilote-Opérateur R. Henrard. 35, 48, 102: Giraudon. 50, 57, 58, 60, 61: A. Trincano (Ed. Arthaud). 63, 64: Claude Arthaud (Ed. Arthaud). 79: H. Adant (Ed. Arthaud). 84: Lapie-Photothèque Française.

Colour plates by: Marc Lavrillier (Ed. Arthaud).

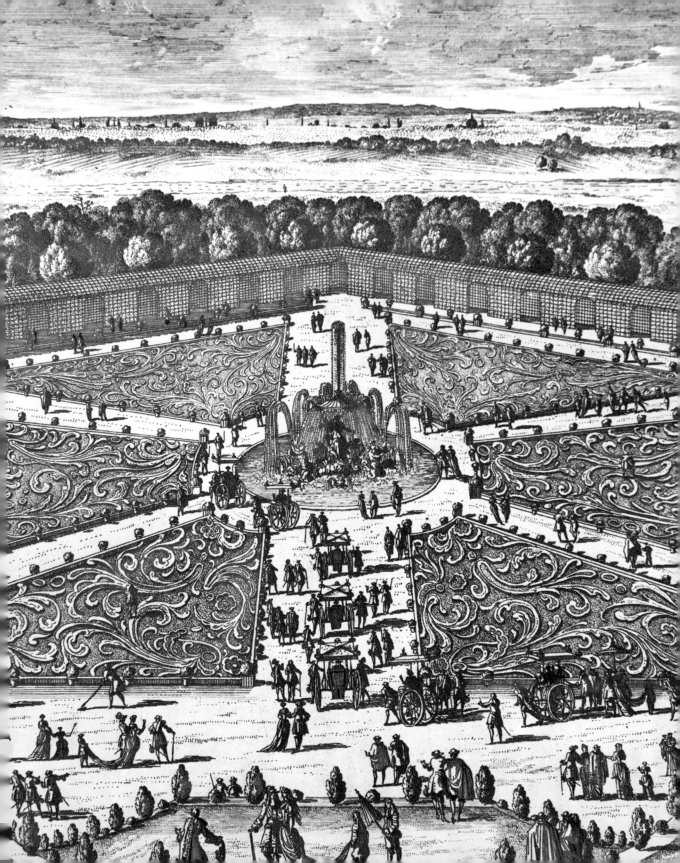

5

8

9

10

11

7. *Le donjon.*
8. *La Sainte-Chapelle.*
9 et 10. *La Sainte-Chapelle.*
    Détails de la frise de la console.
11. *L'Arc de triomphe de Le Vau.*

7. *The keep.*
8. *The chapel.*
9-10. *The chapel. Details from the*
    frieze of the console.
11. *Triumphal arch by Le Vau.*

7. *Der Schlossturm.*
8. *Die Sainte-Chapelle.*
9-10. *Die Sainte-Chapelle. Details*
    des Kragsteinfrieses.
11. *Der Triumphbogen von Le Vau.*

13

12. *Dans le bois de Vincennes.*
13. *Montlhéry. Le donjon.*
14. *La Ferté-Milon. Entrée du château.*

12. *In the Bois de Vincennes.*
13. *Montlhéry. The keep.*
14. *La Ferté-Milon. The main gate.*

12. *Im Wald von Vincennes.*
13. *Montlhéry. Der Schlossturm.*
14. *La Ferté-Milon. Eingang zum Schloss.*

15

15. *Gisors. Le donjon.*
16. *Dourdan. Tours et fossés.*
17. *Pierrefonds. Vue d'ensemble du château.*
18. *Pierrefonds. Statue de Viollet-le-Duc sous les traits de Saint Jacques le Majeur.*

15. *Gisors. The keep.*
16. *Dourdan. Towers and moats.*
17. *Pierrefonds. General view of the castle.*
18. *Pierrefonds. Statue of Viollet-le-Duc as Saint-Jacques le Majeur.*

15. *Gisors. Der Schlossturm.*
16. *Dourdan. Der Schlossgraben.*
17. *Pierrefonds. Gesamtansicht des Schlosses.*
18. *Pierrefonds. Statue, die Viollet-le-Duc als St. Jacques le Majeur darstellt.*

FRANCIS
CVS

FRANCORVM
REX

19

Fontainebleau

22

23

24

25. La salle du Conseil.

26. Les appartements de Marie-Antoinette. Le boudoir.

25. The Counsel Chamber.
26. The rooms of Marie-Antoinette. The boudoir.
27. The Throne Room.

Fontainebleau

27. *La salle du Trône.*

28.   Fontainebleau. *Vue aérienne.*
     Aerial view.
     Luftbild.

Fontainebleau

29

30

Fontainebleau

31

Meudon

34

Meudon

35

36

35. Le château d'après une
    gravure du temps.
36. L'Orangerie.

35. The castle after an
    engraving of that time.
36. The Orangery.

35. Das Schloss nach einem
    zeitgenössischen
    Kupferstich.
36. Die Orangerie.

Façade sur le parc.
Loggia du logis du
Roi.

The façade over-
looking the park.
The loggia of the
Logis du Roi.

Ansicht vom Park
aus.
Loggia der Woh-
nung des Königs.

40

39. *Plafond de l'escalier de la salle des Etats.*
40. *La salamandre de François Ier.*
41. *Salle des Etats. Retable de 1539.*
42. *Vénus au satyre.*
43. *Cheminée des communs. Armes de François Ier.*

39. *The staircase ceiling of the State Room.*
40. *The salamander of François I.*
41. *The State Room. Reredos of 1539.*
42. *Venus with Satyr.*
43. *Chimney with the arms of François I.*

39. *Decke der Treppe im « Saal der Staaten ».*
40. *Der Salamander des Königs François Ier.*
41. *« Saal der Staaten ». Altar von 1539.*
42. *Venus und Satyr.*
43. *Kamin der Nebengebäude. Wappenzeichen des Königs François Ier.*

41

43

Saint-Germain-en-Laye

46

47

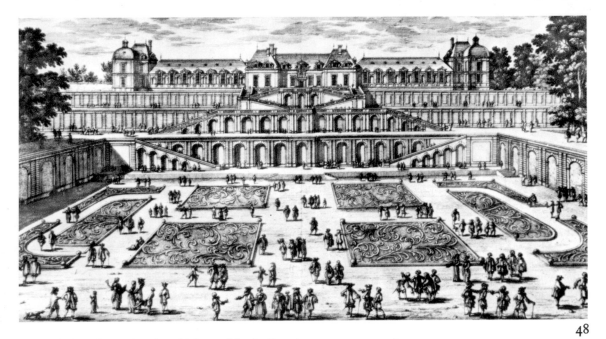

48. *Saint-Germain. Le Château-Neuf d'après une gravure du temps.*
49. *Le château d'Anet d'après une gravure ancienne.*
50. *Anet. Le château vu du parc.*

48. *Saint-Germain. The Château-Neuf from an engraving of that time.*
49. *The castle of Anet after an old engraving.*
50. *Anet. The castle seen from the park.*

48. *Saint-Germain. Das Neue Schloss nach einem zeitgenössischen Kupferstich.*
49. *Das Schloss von Anet nach einem alten Kupferstich.*
50. *Anet. Ansicht des Schlosses vom Park her.*

51

52

53

55. Dallage et autel.
56. La coupole.
57 et 58. Les anges.

55. The altar and paving.
56. The cupola.
57-58. Angels.

55. Steinfussboden und Altar.
56. Die Kuppel.
57-58. Die Engel.

57   58

59

Versailles

66

67

68

69

71

72

73

70 à 73. *Appartements de Louis XV: tapisseries, boiserie et mobilier.*
74. *Le Grand Trianon.*

70-73. Rooms of Louis XV: tapestries, woodwork and furniture.
74. *Le Grand Trianon.*

70-73. Gemächer Ludwigs XV : Wandteppich, Holzschnitzerei und Möbel.
74. Das Grosse Trianon.

75

Marly

82

81. *La Grande Perspective.*
82. *Le pavillon de l'Aurore.*

81. *« La Grande Perspective ».*
82. *The pavilion of Aurore.*

81. *Wasserspiele.*
82. *Der Pavillon der Aurora.*

Chantilly ▶

83. *Vue générale du côté du parc.*
84. *Vue aérienne du château et de la
      terrasse.*

83. *General view from the park.*
84. *Aerial view of the castle and
      terrace.*

83. *Gesamtansicht vom Park her.*
84. *Luftbild vom Schloss und der
      Terrasse.*

85

85. *Les chevaux du tympan des Grandes Ecuries.*
86. *Les Grandes Ecuries.*

85. *Horses on the tympanum of the Great Stables.*
86. *The Great Stables.*

85. *Die Pferde im Torbogen des Grossen Marstalls.*
86. *Der Grosse Marstall.*

87. Le canal.
88. L'île d'Amour.

87. The canal.
88. The Island of Love.

87. Der Kanal.
88. Die Liebesinsel.

89

90

91

92

89 à 94. *Le salon des Singes.*
Détails et ensemble.

The room of the Monkey
Details and general vie

Der Affensalon, Deta
und Gesamtansicht.

93

94

95

96

95. *La maison de Sylvie.*
96 à 99. *Détails des boiseries de la maison
de Sylvie.*

95. *The house of Sylvie.*
96-99. *Details of woodwork in the house
of Sylvie.*

95. *Das Haus Sylvies.*
96-99. *Teilansichten der Holzschnitzereien
im Haus Sylvies.*

97

98

99

*103 et 104. Deux aspec
du parc.*

*Two views of t.
park.*

Im Park.

105 et 108. Le bois de Brimborion, entre Bellevue et Sèvres.

106. Louveciennes.

107. Choisy-le-Roi. Un pavillon.

105-108. The park of Brimborion, between Bellevue and Sèvres.

106

107

106. *Louveciennes.*
107. *Choisy-le-Roi.*
     Pavilion.

105-108. *Der Wald*
     von Brimborion,
     zwischen Belle-
     vue und Sèvres.
106. *Louveciennes.*
107. *Choisy-le-Roi.*
     Ein Pavillon.

108

III. Boiseries de chêne des Appartements d'assemblée.

II2. La Laiterie de la Reine.

111. Carving on the oak doors of the Assembly Rooms.
112. The Queen's dairy.
113. Delft tiling in the bathroom.

111. « Appartements d'assemblée ». Geschnitzte Eichentür.
112. Der Melkraum der Königin.
113. Fayencen von Delft im Baderaum,

113. Faïence de Delft de la salle de Bains.

114. Porte du salon
en rotonde.
115 et 116. Deux as-
pects du pavillon.
117. La rotonde.

114. The door of the
round room.
115-116. Two views
of the pavilion.

115

116

117. The dome of the
      round room.

114. Türe des runden
      Salons.
115-116. Ansichten
      des Pavillons.
117. Kuppel des
      runden Salons.

118

118. *Musée de la Voiture. Salle des carrosses.*
119. *Salle des Colonnes.*
120. *Façade sur le parc.*

118. *Musée de la Voiture. The hall of carriages.*
119. *Hall of pillars.*
120. *The façade overlooking the park.*

118. *Kutschenmuseum. Saal der Karossen.*
119. *Säulensaal.*
120. *Fassade gegen den Park.*

121. *Chambre à coucher de l'Empereur.*

Compiègne

122. *Galerie de Bal.*

123. *Chambre à coucher de l'Impératrice Marie-Louise.*

Malmaison

125

126

Malmaison

127 et 128. Dans la
    bibliothèque.
    Bureau de l'Em-
    pereur et statuette
    de Bonaparte pen-
    dant la campagne
    d'Egypte, par
    Mouton.
129. Le masque mor-
    tuaire de l'Em-
    pereur.

127-128. The Library.
    The Emperor's
    desk and statue of
    Bonaparte during
    the Egyptian cam-
    paign, by Mouton.
129. The death-mask
    of the Emperor.

127-128. In der
    Bibliothek.
    Schreibtisch des
    Kaisers und
    Plastik von Mou-
    ton, Bonaparte
    während der
    Kampagne in
    Ägypten
    darstellend.
129. Die Totenmaske
    des Kaisers.

127